Issues in Student Assessment

Dorothy Bray, *Editor*
College of the Desert

Marcia J. Belcher, *Editor*
Miami–Dade Community College

NEW DIRECTIONS FOR COMMUNITY COLLEGES
ARTHUR M. COHEN, *Editor-in-Chief*
FLORENCE B. BRAWER, *Associate Editor*

Number 59, Fall 1987

Paperback sourcebooks in
The Jossey-Bass Higher Education Series

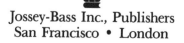

Jossey-Bass Inc., Publishers
San Francisco • London

EDUCATIONAL RESOURCES INFORMATION CENTER

ERIC Clearinghouse For Junior Colleges

UNIVERSITY OF CALIFORNIA, LOS ANGELES

Dorothy Bray, Marcia J. Belcher (eds.).
Issues in Student Assessment.
New Directions for Community Colleges, no. 59.
Volume XV, number 3.
San Francisco: Jossey-Bass, 1987.

New Directions for Community Colleges
Arthur M. Cohen, *Editor-in-Chief;* Florence B. Brawer, *Associate Editor*

New Directions for Community Colleges is published quarterly by Jossey-Bass Inc.,
Publishers (publication number USPS 121-710), in association with the ERIC
Clearinghouse for Junior Colleges. *New Directions* is numbered sequentially—
please order extra copies by sequential number. The volume and issue numbers
above are included for the convenience of libraries. Second-class postage paid at
San Francisco, California, and at additional mailing offices. POSTMASTER: Send
address changes to Jossey-Bass, Inc., Publishers, 433 California Street, San Francisco,
California 94104.

The material in this publication was prepared pursuant to a contract with
the Office of Educational Research and Improvement, U.S. Department of
Education. Contractors undertaking such projects under government sponsorship
are encouraged to express freely their judgment in professional and technical
matters. Prior to publication, the manuscript was submitted to the Center for
the Study of Community Colleges for critical review and determination of
professional competence. This publication has met such standards. Points of view
or opinions, however, do not necessarily represent the official view or opinions of
the Center for the Study of Community Colleges or the Office
of Educational Research and Improvement.

Editorial correspondence should be sent to the Editor-in-Chief, Arthur M. Cohen,
at the ERIC Clearinghouse for Junior Colleges, University of California,
Los Angeles, California 90024.

Library of Congress Catalog Card Number LC 85-644753

International Standard Serial Number ISSN 0194-3081

International Standard Book Number ISBN 1-55542-953-X

Cover art by WILLI BAUM

Manufactured in the United States of America

*Office of Educational
Research and Improvement
U.S. Department of Education*

Ordering Information

The paperback sourcebooks listed below are published quarterly and can be ordered either by subscription or single copy.

Subscriptions cost $52.00 per year for institutions, agencies, and libraries. Individuals can subscribe at the special rate of $39.00 per year *if payment is by personal check.* (Note that the full rate of $52.00 applies if payment is by institutional check, even if the subscription is designated for an individual.) Standing orders are accepted.

Single copies are available at $12.95 when payment accompanies order. (California, New Jersey, New York, and Washington, D.C., residents please include appropriate sales tax.) For billed orders, cost per copy is $12.95 plus postage and handling.

Substantial discounts are offered to organizations and individuals wishing to purchase bulk quantities of Jossey-Bass sourcebooks. Please inquire.

Please note that these prices are for the academic year 1987–88 and are subject to change without notice. Also, some titles may be out of print and therefore not available for sale.

To ensure correct and prompt delivery, all orders must give either the *name of an individual* or an *official purchase order number.* Please submit your order as follows:

Subscriptions: specify series and year subscription is to begin.
Single Copies: specify sourcebook code (such as, CC1) and first two words of title.

Mail orders for United States and Possessions, Australia, New Zealand, Canada, Latin America, and Japan to:
Jossey-Bass Inc., Publishers
433 California Street
San Francisco, California 94104

Mail orders for all other parts of the world to:
Jossey-Bass Limited
28 Banner Street
London EC1Y 8QE

New Directions for Community Colleges Series
Arthur M. Cohen, *Editor-in-Chief*
Florence B. Brawer, *Associate Editor*

Contents

Editor's Notes

Assessment is a potent tool in shaping directions for higher education. Legislators are interested in it. Administrators are mystified by it. Practitioners are challenged by it. Faculty are afraid of it. Students are affected by it. What to do, how to do it, and why it should be done are being asked on many levels. In the 1987 education environment, assessment can be defined as the activities of testing, evaluation, and documentation. Standardized testing is only one of a number of avenues available.

Almost without exception, recent writers on reform in higher education address the issue of assessment. While some place the responsibility with the individual institution, others urge movement at the state level. And movement has occurred. A recent survey of the fifty states found that, while few had formal assessment mechanisms in place at the state level only a year or two ago, two thirds now report that they do if the term *assessment* is not limited to traditional and narrow definitions (Boyer, Ewell, Finney, and Mingle, 1987). In contrast to the mandated statewide testing programs that are typically envisioned for state-level assessment, these authors describe a mosaic of state initiatives that extend assessment initiatives to early intervention programs, incorporate assessment into existing planning and accountability mechanisms, and redefine assessment as including the monitoring of other outcomes, such as student retention and graduate satisfaction. Moreover, most of the state higher education executive officers surveyed believe that assessment plans should be developed locally and that they should reflect the institutional mission.

The current literature discusses community colleges as a component of postsecondary education, subject to the same standards as other institutions. We acknowledge that we cannot discuss assessment for community colleges as separate from the dialogue on assessment for four-year colleges and universities. In fact, community colleges have a particularly urgent mandate to join in the dialogue, shape the assessment models, and present their findings and outcomes to the public. The traditional response to the calls to improve higher education has been to raise entrance standards, and the survey by Boyer, Ewell, Finney, and Mingle (1987) indicates that some states are again considering this response. Community colleges are open-door institutions. If they are to retain their mission, they have the obligation to present other responses to the demands for accountability through assessment.

In a review of state-mandated testing and educational reform, Airasian (1987) considers the new roles being asked of assessment, especially state-mandated assessment. Airasian notes that an emphasis on the technical aspects of testing will not suffice, since the crucial issues are social, economic, and value laden. It is appropriate, then, that the contents of this volume are much more than a how-to guide. The chapters cover three areas of assessment: accountability issues and the political tensions that they reflect; assessment practices, the use and misuse of testing, and emerging directions; and the impact of assessment, which includes issues of student access and opportunity, technological applications, expanded models for assessment, and increased linkages between high schools and colleges as a result of assessment information. Finally, this volume suggests the need to focus on the next challenge: to take assessment beyond its presently politically mandated stages to its rightful purpose—improving the curriculum and the quality of teaching and learning within the institution.

To introduce accountability issues, Daniel Resnick offers a historical perspective on testing and American education. He argues that the tensions and solutions once faced by the public school sector are now being encountered in the arena of higher education. In Chapter Two, Peter M. Hirsch explores the relationship between mandates for educational excellence and increased standards and access to educational opportunity for all students. He underscores the difference between accountability-based assessment and compliance-based testing. In Chapter Three, John Losak argues that rigor in classroom assessment is the only way of reducing outside interference in the assessment process. He recommends that we reduce the role of individual instructors in assessment.

The area of assessment practices covers a wide variety of topics. One approach advocated with increasing frequency but as yet seldom implemented is called *value-added testing*. In Chapter Four, Marcia Belcher synthesizes the arguments for and against such an approach and describes several alternatives. In Chapter Five, Scarvia Anderson examines the assessment method most often used (and abused) in higher education today: the teacher-made test.

Two practices are increasingly common components of the testing arsenal: placement testing and large-scale essay testing. In Chapter Six, Linda Crocker describes ways of overcoming some of the common pitfalls of essay testing and scoring. In Chapter Seven, Edward Morante critiques placement test practices and models and offers guidelines for the development of an appropriate placement testing system, and in Chapter Eight, Emmett Casey discusses ways in which testing practices can be modified to meet the special needs of disabled students.

The last face of assessment considered in this volume reflects the trends that are likely to develop as a result of the increased attention to assessment. Roy McTarnaghan argues in Chapter Nine that assessment does not necessarily affect minorities negatively. In Chapter Ten, Jeanine Rounds, Martha Kanter, and Marlene Blumin consider the impact of emerging Technology on testing, and in Chapter Eleven, Susan Obler and Maureen Ramer point out that the designers of assessment and counseling systems need to consider populations other than recent high school graduates and to envision systems that accommodate individual education planning and career goals. In the concluding chapter, Jim Palmer cites recent publications that address the issues raised in this volume.

The contributors began from the premise that colleges must restore public confidence in their quality and effectiveness. We conclude by suggesting that the effective institution will no longer focus only on assessing its students' abilities but also on using assessment information to improve its curriculum and the quality of the teaching-learning process. In their efforts to restore public confidence through assessment, colleges must appreciate that standardized testing is only one of many tools. Colleges must learn to use assessment to provide information that documents past successes and future needs and that helps to improve the curriculum.

Dorothy Bray
Marcia J. Belcher
Editors

References

Airasian, P. W. "State-Mandated Testing and Educational Reform: Context and Consequences." *American Journal of Education,* 1987, *95* (3), 393–412.

Boyer, C. M., Ewell, P. T., Finney, J. E., and Mingle, J. R. "Assessment and Outcomes Measurement: A View from the States." *AAHE Bulletin,* 1987, *39* (7), 8–12.

Dorothy Bray is vice-president for education services at College of the Desert in Palm Desert, California.

Marcia J. Belcher is senior research associate at Miami–Dade Community College in Miami, Florida.

Student assessment efforts are historically linked to the ebb and flow of public confidence in the nation's schools and colleges.

Expansion, Quality, and Testing in American Education

Daniel P. Resnick

The United States has just completed a momentous expansion of its system of higher education. That expansion was sustained over a period of about thirty years, between 1954 and 1983. During that period, enrollments increased on average close to 6 percent each year and for the first twenty years at an average rate of 7.6 percent (National Center for Education Statistics, 1973, 1985; Bureau of the Census, 1976). Major changes occurred in the postsecondary structure as it grew and adapted to the needs of a growing student population. New kinds of institutions, such as the community colleges, took on an important role. Large state institutions became multiversities, and the liberal arts colleges became increasingly vocationally oriented. The pattern of majors for students shifted, as did the timing and sequence of the years of undergraduate education.

Today, about 3,000 accredited colleges and universities in the United States enroll close to ten million undergraduate students. At the beginning of the expansion, there were about 2,000 accredited colleges and universities and three million undergraduate students. During these three decades, the number of institutions of higher education increased by 50 percent, and the student enrollment *tripled*. By the end of the period of expansion just de-

D. Bray, and M. J. Belcher (eds.). *Issues in Student Assessment.*
New Directions for Community Colleges, no. 59. San Francisco: Jossey-Bass, Fall 1987.

scribed, in academic year 1982-83, national enrollments in each of the major types of postsecondary institution were either holding steady or declining.

The end of expansion poses questions about the future of many institutions. All face problems involved in maintaining enrollments, establishing or sustaining quality programs, securing adequate financing, and maintaining public confidence. The selective institutions—that is, institutions that are able to turn away at least one student for each student accepted—are in the most favored positions, but they are no more than fifty or so in number, and perhaps only half can be more selective (Fiske, 1985). Most institutions of higher education see rather lean years ahead.

The present situation is not yet a crisis, but the problems are real. The supply of places exceeds the demand. A number of institutions have insufficient funds to maintain operations. Large segments of the lay public have little confidence in the quality and effectiveness of higher education. In contrast to the problems of the high schools, the problems of the colleges and universities are not yet at center stage, and there is certainly no consensus on what ought to be done.

Nonetheless, the problems will receive increasing attention in the years ahead. Political actors and scholars are pointing fingers. Secretary of Education William Bennett has called on college and university leaders, first in October 1984 and then on a number of subsequent occasions, to find ways to show the public that their institutions make a valued difference in the education and growth of students. Governors have called on universities and colleges to show their contribution to more efficient learning. Several state legislatures are refusing to maintain funding for state universities and community colleges without prior demonstrations that current subsidies have been used effectively. In his examination of a number of recent studies of undergraduate education, Hacker (1986) expressed a similar doubt about the quality and effectiveness of higher education.

How can we gain perspective on these developments? To students of American higher education, the current problems have a familiar ring because they suggest the problems that followed the half century of expansion of the system of secondary education in the United States in the period between 1890 and 1935. During that period enrollments increased on average almost 8 percent each year, with a peak close to 9 percent in the years between 1909 and 1924. The number of public high school diplomas awarded increased on average 7.9 percent each year during that period; in the peak years, the average increase was 9.8 percent (Bureau of the Census, 1976). Although there are obvious differences between institutions of secondary education and institutions of higher education, we propose this analogy because there are common features in the pressures behind expansion in the two periods: certain common features in the kinds of transformations undergone by educational institutions, certain common problems in maintaining the confidence of the public in the quality and effectiveness of changing institutions, and certain common strategies for maintaining this confidence. At the same time, the comparison makes us aware that the problems of higher education today are distinctive and that they require new remedies. The analogy is imperfect but useful.

During this period of rapid expansion between 1890 and 1935, the United States became the first Western nation to bring a substantial portion of its school-age population into secondary schools. France, Germany, and Great Britain did not begin a comparable expansion until after the Second World War (Heidenheimer, 1973). The rate of expansion of the secondary schools then exceeded the increase in the school-eligible population, which had been swollen during most of that period by the heaviest immigration rates in our history (Wagner, 1971). As scholars have argued, the commitment to schooling was driven by a belief in education as a source of moral improvement, common to both Protestant and rationalist traditions in our society (Welter, 1962).

In 1890, it can be estimated that fewer than 15 percent of the fourteen- to seventeen-year-olds in our society were in high schools. By 1935, the figure had leaped to more than 70 percent. In 1890, little more than 6 percent of the seventeen- and eighteen-year-olds completed high school. By 1935, almost half of those in that age group had done so (Bureau of the Census, 1976). During these years, the costs of school construction and teacher salaries were largely and increasingly borne by local homeowners in communities across America.

The schools became less selective during this period. The disappearance of the entrance examination to the high school was one important sign of this development: Maintained by most of the public high schools in 1900, the entrance examination had disappeared almost entirely by 1925. High school entrance examinations were incompatible with the mission of opening the doors to all who were interested in continuing their education. During this period, there also developed a pattern of promotion from class to class for entire age groups that was relatively independent of the mastery of school subjects. The older pattern of promotion by merit was rejected as costly, inefficient, and out of harmony with the commitment to education growth (Ayres, 1909).

School programs adapted to the new waves of students, introducing subject matter that was believed to meet student interests more than the established programs of history, geography, literature, classics (languages, literature, philosophy), science, and mathematics. Vocational subjects entered the curriculum, along with a variety of other courses that were considered part of a general program and not as preparation for college. The *Cardinal Principles of Secondary Education* (National Education Association of the United States, 1918) provided a rationale for the new vocationalism, just as the Report of the Committee of Ten (Sizer, 1964) had provided programmatic support for the traditional curriculum.

A major new institution was created in this period, the comprehensive high school. Within its walls gathered students with very different programs—some remaining four years, others dropping out earlier; some headed for the trades, others for college. They would meet in a common homeroom class before dispersing for very different and varied educational experiences. A major casualty of this new pattern of education was the core curriculum. Students were brought together for elements of a common social experience, not a common academic program.

Public confidence in the effectiveness of the high schools was shaken by the knowledge that students who would formerly have failed high school entrance examinations could now enter freely. It was also the case that testing of 1.7 million military recruits in World War I revealed a large number of near illiterates who had attended American high schools (Yerkes, 1921; Brigham, 1923). In response, school principals and superintendents in the 70,000 or so school districts across the country made an important effort after World War I through their professional associations and their individual efforts within school systems to show that they were managing their expanding systems efficiently. Extolling their testing programs, they argued that scientific procedures were being used to place students in appropriate programs and that the effectiveness of the different instructional programs was being regularly assessed. The chosen instrument for this scientific assessment was the standardized objective multiple-choice test (Resnick, 1982).

In the period between 1912 and 1922, school testing bureaus were created in nine of the ten largest city school districts in the United States, and by 1925, there were sixty such bureaus across the country. These bureaus ordered, administered, and interpreted tests in their school districts. In response to a survey in 1925, they reported that the major use of aptitude tests was to place students in homogeneously grouped classes (Bureau of Education, 1926; Deffenbaugh, 1923, 1926). Achievement tests were used to assess the effectiveness of programs within individual schools and to compare the performance of different schools.

The fact that results on achievement tests were published in local newspapers and that aptitude tests were widely used to defend decisions about classroom placement and educational guidance indicates two points of great importance. First, educators were very sensitive about their relations with parents and community leaders. They recognized the importance of remaining accountable for their conduct to the community of parents and taxpayers. Second, they found that decisions that could be supported by test results were generally assumed to be sound. Tests appeared to be impartial, objective, and scientific. For lay people, the results were difficult to contest.

Like the first expansion, the more than threefold increase in postsecondary undergraduate enrollments between 1954 and 1983 was driven in part by demographic factors and in part by the increased importance assigned in the workplace and society at large to additional years of education. Not quite half of the increase can be attributed to the baby boom. The rest came from an increase in the portion of the youth cohort that attended college. As in the first expansion, America was the first Western nation to offer so many years of education to her young people. The first expansion that we are examining here was aimed principally at those between the ages of fourteen and eighteen; the second, at those between eighteen and twenty-four.

This second expansion brought changes in the structures of higher education, as the first expansion had brought changes in the structure of the high schools. One major change was the dramatic sevenfold growth in the number of community colleges: By 1983 about 1,450 two-year institutions were in place. As these institutions grew in number, their enrollments kept pace. More than 40 percent of the close to ten million undergraduate students in 1983 were in two-year community colleges, as compared with 14 percent in 1960. These students tended to be part-time, vocationally oriented, and relatively unlikely to complete a four-year degree.

As undergraduates sought their degrees in different kinds of institutions and as new kinds of students entered these structures, the academic programs that students pursued also changed character, even in the traditional four-year institution. A core curriculum in traditional subjects gave way to a variety of vocational offerings. Analysis of National Center for Education Statistics (1985) data on baccalaureate degrees awarded between 1963 and 1983 indicates that the portion of students who majored in history, social science, literature, foreign languages, philosophy, math, and science declined precipitously, from about 40 percent to 20 percent of majors. At the same time, business majors almost doubled as a portion of baccalaureate recipients, receiving 23 percent of the degrees.

Just as growth in public funding was critical for the secondary schools during their period of expansion, colleges and universities became more dependent on public funding during their expansion. The greatest single beneficiaries of enrollments in the second period of growth were the state and community colleges, which depended largely on state legislatures for support.

This second period of expansion has been a difficult one in which to maintain public confidence in institutions of higher learning. The nation is still emerging from an intense period of criticism of its secondary institutions that produced more than a dozen commission reports and an indictment of a "rising tide of mediocrity." The public recognizes that the products of these secondary schools are entering higher education. How good are the institutions that receive these graduates?

Even as confidence in the quality and effectiveness of institutions of higher learning has waned, the cost of schooling has risen more rapidly than the rate of inflation. And, unemployment and underemployment among young graduates has brought into question the ability of a college degree to assure integration into the work force. At the same time, the nation faces demands for increased military appropriations and continuing support of domestic entitlement programs in a period of unsettling fiscal problems. These are difficult times in which to restore confidence in the quality of our institutions of higher learning.

But, our colleges and universities must act to restore public confidence. The recruitment of students, federal and state subsidies, foundation support, and even research contracts depend on the implied and preliminary contract of confidence. Four kinds of action are likely. The first two employ the time-honored techniques of our market society and democratic political system. The last two invoke strategies associated with the movement for assessment in higher education.

The first response can be described as marketing, directed through a variety of media to publics of parents and potential students. The second is lobbying, in which public colleges and universities, along with private institutions seeking public support for research and other purposes, make their claims before legislators, departments of education, and other agencies. The third response, testing, calls on a form of assessment whose first educational uses were in primary and secondary schools. Standardized tests are now used in some colleges and universities to establish minimum competency for admission, promotion, or graduation. The expectation is that the scientific nature of the procedure will satisfy external demands for accountability. The fourth response is still emerging. It, too, belongs with the current assessment movement. It calls on colleges and universities to devise their own evaluation instruments, appropriate to their specific missions, student bodies, and academic programs. Although the primary clients for the resulting evaluations are the institution's administration, faculty, and board of trustees, it is expected that these results, like those from competency testing, will also be communicated to a wider public.

Standardized testing was used from the early 1920s by primary and secondary schools mainly to develop public confidence in placement decisions and to assess programs. Secondary schools in a number of city and state systems gave it a new use in the late 1960s and 1970s at a time of contest over the behavior, learning, and course programs of secondary school students. Tests that were standardized on a statewide basis were developed to serve as measures of high school exit-level competency and make the diploma a certification that the high school graduate had certain minimum skills in reading and math. More than two thirds of the states had imposed minimum competency tests by the mid 1980s (Resnick, 1980; Ericson, 1984).

Colleges and universities had used standardized intelligence tests for admissions screening since the early 1920s, in some instances to impose quotas against minorities (Wechsler, 1977). In 1926, Carl Brigham introduced the Scholastic Aptitude Test (SAT) for the College Board. The SAT drew on verbal and mathematical aptitudes in a multiple-choice mode; it was not widely used until after World War II. But, in the past forty years it has become the most heavily used test of the College Board and, with the American College Test (ACT), the major entrance screening device used by institutions of higher education. During the same period, the multiple-choice mode was imposed for almost all subject matter testing of college applicants. The results of those tests were used for placement and to grant credit or exemption.

Competency testing in the high schools, which began in the late 1960s, created an acceptability for system- and statewide efforts to certify minimum levels of ability in reading, writing, and math among students in public institutions. In the early and mid 1980s, demands for competency testing were extended to colleges and universities. Florida, New Jersey, and Tennessee led the way in imposing mandated competency testing programs. Such testing was used to place students with low levels of verbal and mathematical skills in remedial tracks, to monitor entry-level qualifications for students transferring from two-year to four-year colleges, to establish minimum competencies for graduation from four-year public institutions, and in some instances to provide grounds for the reallocation of financial resources within a statewide university system.

State legislatures demanded demonstrations of gains in achievements. They wanted to see gains in learning by students during their undergraduate years, and they wanted to see them measured by standardized tests. The public became accustomed to seeing standardized testing used as a measure of educational performance by institutions during the expansion of our secondary education system. They appreciated its scientific character—objectivity in grading, reliability of results, effective use of technology, simplicity—results that could be reduced to a single score; and its economy—low per-unit cost for each administration. They also liked the possibility of comparing the performance of one group with the performance of populations elsewhere.

To measure achievement, the legislatures wanted achievement tests. Such tests could be provided statewide for basic math and reading skills when the curriculum was adapted to teach what the tests measured. But, unless a curriculum was created for the tests, it was impossible to expect the measures to measure achievement, even when they were labeled achievement tests. Given the variety and diversity of our institutions of higher learning, the variety of textbooks, and the different ways in which faculty had been trained, there was no residual common curriculum. This core had been fragmented in the colleges and universities, as it had earlier been fragmented in the high schools. Statewide achievement measures were possible for minimum skills in specific areas where the tests actually prescribed the curriculum. It was not possible for other kinds of skills and knowledge.

When broader measures of performance were sought, legislators and educators had to turn to aptitude tests. Aptitude measures, which used some variant of the verbal and mathematical sections in the group intelligence tests introduced to elementary and secondary schools in the 1920s, had the great merit of not being tied to any specific curriculum. Indeed, they were respected in the 1920s because it was presumed that they did not discriminate against those who had been exposed to courses of very different character and quality. They were justified by some as somehow equalizing the differences between weak schools and strong ones and as allowing native abilities to triumph over poor environment.

In the 1920s, many psychologists believed that native aptitudes predicted success in school, on the job, and in later life. Few share such beliefs in the 1980s. In place of a belief in the determining role in life of natural gifts and heredity, most Americans believe that hard work is the major determinant of success. Aptitude testing has been inherited from a period in which American elites shared different values. It has persisted for so long because we have not found other reliable predictors of future performance that permit us to compare populations in our many and varied educational institutions.

Reliance on aptitude tests in the 1980s is fraught with problems. Aptitude tests still permit national comparisons of performance by populations with very different kinds of educational experience. And, to the degree that they measure knowledge and skills that are independent of what is taught and learned in specific courses and curriculums, they control for differences in school experience. However, performance on such measures is strongly dependent on socioeconomic background, and it is far from culture-free. Such performance privileges family background, not hard work. Few can now accept that this kind of assessment is equitable.

Aptitude tests were not designed to measure college achievement. To measure such achievement, we will need reliable measures of learning gains on available local curricula. Such tests will have a classroom-based curricular validity that nationally standardized achievement measures do not have. But, they are not likely to permit the kinds of comparisons of performance among institutions that nationally normed instruments make possible. Will it ever be possible to develop tests that have curricular validity and yet provide bases for comparisons nationally? This is a challenge for test developers that requires them to pay equal attention to what is taught and to what is learned in college and university classrooms.

Key foundations, professional associations, and the Department of Education are leading the search for new ways of measuring learning gains in higher education. They are joined by a number of institutions engaging in their own experimentation, sometimes collaboratively, with or without external support. The American Association for Higher Education, with support from the Fund for the Improvement of Post-Secondary Education (FIPSE), has become a clearinghouse for information about current projects.

In his recent study of tensions in undergraduate institutions, Boyer

(1987) has underlined the importance of ongoing assessment in the baccalaureate college. The Carnegie Foundation for the Advancement of Teaching is funding my own ongoing study of assessment issues in historical and policy perspective. Adelman (1986) provides a useful introduction to assessment issues. Bok (1986) makes the case for active involvement in assessment by already strong institutions. Bok has joined FIPSE in funding a three-year study of assessment in higher education led by Richard Light of the Kennedy School. Faculty and administrators from nearby Ivy League colleges and universities have joined Harvard colleagues in working groups on a variety of assessment projects. The Association of American Colleges has received support from FIPSE for a three-year study of pilot projects that seek to strengthen academic programs in eighteen colleges and universities.

The effort to build public confidence in higher education will focus public attention on the curricula of institutions of higher learning, and it may help our colleges to rebuild appropriate cores of learning in harmony with their educational goals. However, this program of reconstruction is a long-term project. In the short term, the response of the great majority of America's colleges and universities to a loss of confidence will be more vigorous marketing efforts and increased lobbying for support from public bodies. At the same time, many institutions will have to show their accountability to state legislatures on common competency tests, which are little adapted to reveal the goals and strengths of different campuses. Only a small number of colleges and universities can be expected to lead the way in developing new measures of assessment that are appropriate to the variety of our postsecondary institutions.

Until there is more research, very little can be said about how students change and grow in the varied settings that have taken shape during the expansion of higher education. A small core of careful research and a number of personal intuitions complement shared experiences. What has been reported to date is not enough to dispel the current skepticism. When the research and reconstruction program of the next decade has produced results, the task of maintaining high levels of public funding for these institutions may be easier than it is now. But, even with research that can show the value added by college, there will be no easy victory. The excess capacity of our postsecondary institutions, the nation's economic and budgetary problems, and the decline of public confidence in the preparation for college given by public secondary schools all suggest that the current problem of confidence is likely to persist for some time.

References

Adelman, C. (ed.). *Assessment in American Higher Education: Issues and Contexts.* Washington, D.C.: Office of Educational Research and Improvement, 1986.

Ayres, L. P. *Laggards in Our Schools: A Study of Retardation and Elimination in City School Systems.* New York: Russell Sage Foundation, 1909.

Bok, D. "Education of Qual'ty." *Harvard Magazine,* 1986, *88* (5), 49–64.

Boyer, E. *The Undergraduate Experience.* New York: Harper & Row, 1987.

Brigham, C. *A Study of American Intelligence.* Princeton, N.J.: Princeton University Press, 1923.

Bureau of Education. *Cities Reporting the Use of Homogeneous Grouping and of the Winnetka Technique and the Dalton Plan.* U.S. Bureau of Education City School Leaflet no. 22. Washington, D.C.: U.S. Department of the Interior, 1926.

Bureau of the Census. *Historical Statistics of the United States: Colonial Times to 1970.* Washington, D.C.: U.S. Government Printing Office, 1976.

Deffenbaugh, W. S. *Research Bureaus in City School Systems.* Washington, D.C.: U.S. Department of Interior, 1923.

Deffenbaugh, W. S. *Uses of Intelligence and Achievement Tests in 215 Cities.* U.S. Bureau of Education City School Leaflet no. 20. Washington, D.C.: U.S. Department of the Interior, 1926.

Ericson, D. "Of Minima and Maxima: The Social Significance of Minimal Competency Testing and the Search for Educational Excellence." *American Journal of Education,* 1984, *92* (3), 245–261.

Fiske, E. B. *Selective Guide to Colleges 1984–85.* New York: Times Books, 1985.

Hacker, A. "The Decline of Higher Learning." *New York Review of Books,* 1986, *33* (2), 35–44.

Heidenheimer, A. J. "The Politics of Public Education, Health, and Welfare in the USA and Western Europe: How Growth and Reform Potentials Have Differed." *British Journal of Political Science,* 1973, *3,* 315–340.

National Center for Education Statistics. *Digest of Education Statistics, 1972 Edition.* Washington, D.C.: U.S. Government Printing Office, 1973.

National Center for Education Statistics. *Condition of Education, 1985 Edition.* Washington, D.C.: U.S. Government Printing Office, 1985.

National Education Association of the United States. *Cardinal Principles of Secondary Education.* Washington, D.C.: U.S. Government Printing Office, 1918.

Resnick, D. P. "Minimum Competency Testing Historically Considered." In D. C. Berliner (ed.), *Review of Research in Education.* Washington, D.C.: American Educational Research Association, 1980.

Resnick, D. P. "History of Educational Testing." In A. Widgor and W. Garner (eds.), *Ability Testing: Uses, Consequences, and Controversies.* Part II. Washington, D.C.: National Research Council, 1982.

Sizer, T. *Secondary Schools at the Turn of the Century.* New Haven, Conn.: Yale University Press, 1964.

Wagner, P. *The Distant Magnet: European Immigration to the U.S.A.* New York: Harper & Row, 1971.

Wechsler, D. *The Qualified Student: A History of Selective College Admission in America.* New York: Wiley, 1977.

Welter, R. *Popular Education and Democratic Thought in America.* New York: Columbia University Press, 1962.

Yerkes, R. (ed.). *Memoirs of the National Academy of Sciences,* Vol. 40, Part 2: *Psychological Examining in the United States Army.* Washington, D.C.: U.S. Government Printing Office, 1921.

Daniel P. Resnick is professor of history at Carnegie-Mellon University.

Community colleges will be asked to respond to calls for increased educational excellence while maintaining access to educational opportunity for students who are least prepared to succeed. Accountability-based assessment rather than compliance-based testing will be required to accomplish this task.

The Other Side of Assessment

Peter M. Hirsch

From the earliest times, the focus of human thought has been to understand, explain, and predict the world in which we live. With the dawning of civilization, our ancestors' efforts began to transcend the banding that enabled them to survive a natural environment that was both hostile and dangerous. To overcome our physical limitations, we learned to live in groups and in ways that divided the labors of life into manageable and knowable tasks. If we were successful in placing the right persons in the right roles and if we were not overwhelmed by others who did a better job of assessment and placement, our societies survived.

As we learned to control nature, our numbers grew, and our societies became larger and more complex. Role specialization increased, and we developed economic, political, religious, and social structures to create the order that was needed for the many to live together successfully. Gradually, the increasing complexity produced formalized systems for preparing persons to assume their roles. Knowledge acquired value, and schooling and education became necessary parts of the preparation.

Today, American society faces even greater challenges in preparing individuals for successful participation. The information explosion, the enormous influx of immigrants and the new cultural diversity that they create, the transition within our economy from a national to an international base, the shift in employment opportunities from production to services, and the increased role of technology in our daily lives have made

D. Bray, and M. J. Belcher (eds.). *Issues in Student Assessment.*
New Directions for Community Colleges, no. 59. San Francisco: Jossey-Bass, Fall 1987.

advanced formal education essential in America—not for some but for all. The need for an effective and responsive education system has become so crucial that several recent major national reports have addressed the question of how our education systems can be strengthened to meet the challenges facing our society.

The Lure of Reform

Report after report calls for reform of American education. The spiral of public education opportunity, which historically in this nation swirls between access and quality, has once again turned to increased expectations and heightened standards of student performance as the answer to the problems of educating Americans.

Of the recent reports, that of the Study Group on the Conditions of Excellence in American Higher Education (1984) has been most widely quoted. Its position is quite clear; institutions should be accountable for stating their expectations and standards. The Commission for Educational Quality (1985) is even more emphatic. In their view, the quality and meaning of undergraduate education has fallen to the point that mere access has lost much of its value.

Each of us is susceptible to the lure of reform. It is a glamorous topic that has the face advantage of providing simple answers to complex questions. Yet, with an overburdened K-12 system and the documented underpreparedness not only of the new majority and the economically less well off but of the middle class as well, the problems of access and success, of standards and quality will be intimately interconnected as America's postsecondary education structures move into the twenty-first century.

The Role of Community Colleges

There is no doubt that community colleges will be the first institutions within the postsecondary education tier to count a majority of minorities among their student bodies. In California, many elementary and secondary schools already enroll a majority of minorities. For example, more than eighty languages are spoken by students enrolled in the Los Angeles Unified School District. And, community colleges in California, such as Compton and Los Angeles Southwest, already count a vast majority of minorities among their students. Nor are these developments limited to central Los Angeles. In Alameda, Orange, and San Francisco counties, indeed across the state, community colleges are becoming the port of entry to higher education for increasing numbers of the new majority and the traditional poor. In its draft report on California community college reform, the Joint Committee for Review of the Master Plan for Higher Education (1986) estimated that, of the roughly 32 million persons expected to reside in California, by the turn of the century, 52 percent of the school-age children will be minorities, and within the first decade of the twenty-first century, the majority of Californians will represent minority populations. The implications of the demographic data are inescapable: California will be a new majority state. The question is not whether but when. It is equally certain that other states will see similar developments.

In the larger domains of the economy and the quality of life, they are the community colleges that will serve the needs of the new majority and the traditional poor, adult learners and women returning to the classroom, and workers seeking the skills newly required for employment. The community colleges will enable these individuals and others to become fully participating members of our economic, political, and societal fabric.

Indeed, community colleges are the central pivot point in a public education infrastructure designed to enable each person to realize his or her individual potential, to achieve a quality of life that nurtures family and community, and to participate successfully in the labor force. Only if these objectives are achieved for all—fifth-week as well as fifth-generation—will America be able to retain its pre-eminence among nations and continue to compete effectively in the international marketplace. Community colleges will play a key role in accomplishing these objectives. Their ability to do so will be directly related to their ability to demonstrate accountability in maintaining access while achieving the reforms that have been called for.

The Question of Accountability

Partly in response to the work of the Commission on Instruction (1984) of the California Association of Community Colleges, the state of California established a citizen commission to review the state's master plan for higher education. In completing the first part of its review, the California State Commission for the Review of the Master Plan (1986, pp. 1-2) noted that, while the colleges had succeeded beyond all expectations in providing low-cost access, "access must be meaningful, and to be meaningful, it must be access to a quality system that helps ensure the success of every student who enrolls. The responsibility for this success falls on all who participate . . . There must be a commitment on all sides—from the state, from the colleges, and from the students—to excellence and accountability. It is to this end that we urge change."

The emphasis on access, excellence, and accountability is neither new nor recent with respect to American higher education. What is new is the repeated statement, in all recent state and national reports, that access is meaningless without accountability. However, accountability is all too often equated with compliance. This is especially true of the laws enacted by state legislatures and the Congress and of the regulations that state and federal officials develop to implement these laws. One cannot help but ask why?

Figure 1. Characteristic Differences Between Compliance Systems and Accountability Systems

Compliance Systems	*Accountability Systems*
Structured via prescription and proscriptions	Structured to accomplish outcomes and results
Controls-oriented	Goals and objectives–oriented
Promotes status quo	Promotes change
Does not accept ambiguous results	Views ambiguity as a positive force for change
Promotes inclusive management	Promotes management by exception
• Hierarchical control	• Network coordination
• Top-down	• Field-based
• Delegates responsibility	• Delegates authority
• Creates rules and expects them to be followed	• Creates processes to promote participation and involvement
• Punishes failure	• Rewards accomplishments
• Views the system as closed	• Views the system as open and fluid
Uses reporting systems	Uses information systems
• Is descriptive	• Is analytical
• Focuses on rules	• Focuses on issues and problems
• Relies on data	• Uses information
• Seeks minutia	• Seeks trends
• Restricts access to data	• Makes information available
• Data out-of-date as rules change	• Information is futures oriented; its currency is independent of time

Figure 2. Characteristics of America's Best-Run Companies

- A bias for action
- Organizational fluidity

- Customer orientation

- Empowers employees
- Fewer managers, more operators
- Insistence on employee initiative
- Good leadership, not overly managed
- Intense communication systems

- Promotes experimentation
- Promotes autonomy and entrepreneurship among employees

- Tailors products and services to the customer base
- Tolerates failure
- "Don't Write Reports. Do It"

- Objectives that are meaningful to employees
- Views structure as an extended family
- Focuses on priorities supported by shared values

Source: Peters and Waterman (1982).

The answer begins to emerge when we examine the differences between the logic of accountability systems and the logic of compliance systems. Figure 1 contrasts the characteristics of compliance systems and accountability systems. The lists are not meant to be exhaustive but merely suggestive of the differences.

The characteristics of accountability systems listed in Figure 1 are not unlike the characteristics of America's best-run companies that Peters and Waterman (1982) have identified. Figure 2 lists the characteristics of America's best-run companies.

If we compare the two lists, it seems clear that systems of accountability and systems of excellence share the same fundamental characteristics: a bias for action and change based on processes that allow for differences among participants; that tolerate failure and reward success; that promote autonomy, entrepreneurship, and initiative; that share information; and that seek objectives that are meaningful to those involved.

Comparison of the two lists also makes it clear that the characteristics of compliance systems are in direct conflict with the characteristics of America's best-run companies. Where accountability systems seek and promote excellence, compliance systems develop and implement minimum standards. In short, where accountability systems engage individuals to do and be all that they can do and be, compliance systems demand that individuals do and be what they are told to do and be—no more and no less.

Minimum Standards, Testing, and Assessment

In its report on transforming the state role in undergraduate education, the Education Commission of the States (1986) advances eight challenges facing undergraduate education and makes twenty-two recommendations to state leaders for dealing with the challenges that it has identified. The report is directed at how states and state leaders can create a positive environment for institutional leaders in the hope it will contribute significantly to national discussions and to state action.

The most significant and unique feature of this document is the consistent use of accountability as the basis of argument and the concomitant emphasis on assessment rather than on testing: "The term *assessment* is being used to refer to all sorts of activities, from testing basic skills of freshmen to certifying graduates' minimum competencies, from evaluating academic programs to judging whole institutions . . . The terms *testing* and *assessment* often are used interchangeably, which further complicates an already complicated issue . . . assessment has also become a major concern of state leaders. To date, they have been most concerned about enforcing minimum standards for student progress and using standardized tests as tangible evidence that undergraduate education does make a difference . . . But, testing is not synonymous with assessment, nor should it be . . . Standardized tests have some particularly serious drawbacks" (Education Commission of the States, 1986, p. 4).

The Education Commission of the States (1986) report cites the following as limitations of testing and standardized tests: "To evaluate undergraduate education solely on the basis of minimum competence contradicts its very purposes. The outcomes must include knowledge, skills, and attitudes that go far beyond basic skills" (p. 9). "The standardized tests that several states have used to assess system effectiveness were not designed for that purpose . . . Qualitative data must be considered as well as quantitative data" (p. 9). "The need to assess student and institutional performance in ways that improve teaching and learning is not reflected in current efforts" (p. 4). "Screening should not be confused with assessment as a means of improving teaching and learning. To document performance is not to improve performance" (p. 9).

In response to these limitations, the panel makes a number of recommendations. Collectively, the recommendations lay out a strategic plan for integrating assessment into the total process of evaluating student and institutional outcomes. The plan includes the establishment of "early assessment" programs to determine the readiness of high school students for college work and to identify high-risk students and the help that they need in order to stay in school and be successful; the development of special assessment programs, including guidance and counseling, for assessing the educational needs both of returning and of new students, especially those who might be classified as nontraditional; the use of multiple indicators of effectiveness (student demography, program diversity, adequacy of instructional learning resources, student preparation for college work, student participation and completion rates, student satisfaction and placement, alumni and employer satisfaction, work force development, and overall student educational attainment) to evaluate systemwide outcomes; and the encouragement of institutions to develop their own indicators of effectiveness to reflect their distinctive undergraduate education mission, including student participation and completion rates, measures of student-faculty interaction, faculty contribution to the improvement of undergraduate education, student performance within and among majors, writing samples, senior projects, student satisfaction and placement, alumni and employer satisfaction, and faculty development activities.

Assessment and Accountability

Without assessment there can be no accountability. At the same time, without accountability the states and their colleges cannot know whether assessment programs and services are achieving intended purposes. However, the implementation of accountable assessment programs requires deliberate actions at both state and college levels.

At the state level, the governor, the legislature, and the governing boards must first concur on the purposes of assessment. Without this essential agreement, it will not be possible for the colleges to demonstrate accountability in meeting expectations for outcomes. Second, the breadth and depth of the services needed to achieve these identified purposes must be established, and what the colleges will be asked to provide must be clearly understood. Unless this is done, the colleges will not be able to implement appropriate programs of service and referral, nor will they be able to communicate the information to the state that justifies the allocation of funds. Third, outcomes expectations must be clearly defined for the assessment programs and services that the colleges provide, and these expectations must be consistent both with the funding that is provided and with the purposes that have been agreed on for assessment. Fourth, accountability criteria must be developed to provide the structure necessary for implementing assessment programs and services. Colleges are thus free to achieve desired outcomes in ways best suited to the populations that they serve. Minimum standards, which by their very nature can do no more than provide a floor for the delivery of programs and services, are excluded in favor of systems of review that look at the performance of the colleges in meeting the criteria. Fifth, funding must be provided at a level that makes it possible to do the job that needs to be done. Colleges must be authorized to provide a variety of structures through which assessment programs can be delivered, and they must be funded sufficiently to provide such alternatives. Where appropriate staffing to implement state-level assessment purposes is lacking, additional funding must be allocated for staff development of existing personnel and for the recruitment of additional staff. Sixth, the state education code must support the purposes and outcomes that have been agreed on. Existing sections of the education code that are compliance based or that restrict the colleges' freedom to structure their assessment programs in the best interests of the students and communities that they serve must be replaced with code sections that base the evaluation of program success on accountability.

At the college level, boards of trustees, administrations, faculties, and staffs must first establish an institutional climate in which assessment is viewed as a broadly based instructional and student planning and evaluation process. In general, accountable assessment programs are integrated into the total educational program; they are viewed as part and parcel of a single purpose. Second, a broad-based student assessment program must become an integral part of the delivery of instruction at all levels authorized—remedial, developmental, and college-level. At a minimum, the assessment program must include aptitude, career, skills, and self-concept assessment instruments and techniques of sufficient variety to ensure that the full range of students who are likely to enroll can be assessed. Where appropriate college capabilities are lacking, students must be referred to assessment programs external to the college. Third, students' success expectancies must be based on locally normed assessment scores in relation to remedial and developmental program components and college-level courses. Student demographic information must be taken into account. Use of a single standardized test must be avoided, as must reliance solely on standardized tests. Standardized tests are notorious for their lack of cohort reliability both between cohorts in a given time frame and across time frames for a given cohort. In addition, the range of the different combinations of correct and incorrect answers to questions can produce like scores on standardized assessment instruments. Hence, all students who score the same on the same subpart of a given standardized test do not have the same skills strengths and weaknesses. Writing samples and similar college-based assessment tools in mathematics and oral communications must be used as supplements to standardized tests. Fourth, evaluation and student follow-up must become an integral part of the design of the assessment program. Such evaluations and follow-up must examine the effectiveness of the various program components in order to ascertain which assessment instruments predict what program results for which groups of students under what circumstances and conditions. Fifth, assessment information must be used to make curriculum decisions that accommodate students' differing learning styles. Sixth, college support to ensure the success of the assessment program must be made available through funding and staff development opportunities that prepare administrators, counselors, faculty, and support staff both to implement and to evaluate assessment services. This support must be enhanced through the development and implementation of policies and procedures that are supportive of student access to and success in education programs of substance and high quality at every level of instruction. Without the basic institutional support that these factors represent, the desired outcomes of the college's assessment program are likely to remain objectives.

The Other Side of Assessment

In short, the Education Commission of the States (1986) recommendations prescribe state-level and collegewide agreement on the purposes, levels of service, and expected outcomes of assessment programs; funding sufficient to allow the accomplishment of goals and objectives; flexibility to meet local differences in student needs as determined by demographics; and supportive state education code and college policy and procedure language that emphasizes the accomplishment of results, not program structuring and service delivery.

Clearly, the Education Commission of the States panel views assessment as a broadly based system to ascertain student readiness for college work; to provide students, counselors, instructors, and others with the information necessary for ensuring student success; to allow individual colleges to know for whom and how they have been effective; and to enable state education systems to gauge the extent to which students are being served and state priorities are being met. Clearly, this effort goes beyond student performance testing and screening and beyond minimum standards.

But, just as clearly, even the best and most comprehensive assessment program will ultimately be constrained from accomplishing its objectives if it results in a denial of access. This is not simply a matter of individual educational opportunity. In a world where the leading edge of technology changes daily, the future of this nation and its citizens depends on the ability of our education systems to prepare each and every one of us to participate effectively.

This, then, is the other side of assessment: It is the capability of our colleges to be accountable for the purposes for which programs of assessment are conducted. It is the capability of our colleges to enable student success while maintaining access to meaningful educational opportunity for a citizenry characterized by an increasing diversity of culture and skills readiness to participate effectively in the American educational structure. It is the capability of our colleges to demonstrate their effectiveness under conditions of underfunding and the often different educational objectives of states, their public colleges, and the citizens who enroll. It is ultimately, more than anything else, the capability of our colleges to meet each person on his or her terms, to assess his or her individual educational needs, career and life goals, and objectives and to be in a position to provide programs of education that are appropriate and relevant to those needs, goals, and objectives.

And so we come full circle. The ancients labored to control the environment so as to better ensure their futures. As they developed knowledge, they turned to magic to bring powers they did not have to their aid through procedures that ensured outcomes. In short, they endeavored to make the unknown predictable. Today, we labor under similar circumstances—to control the educational process so as to better ensure the futures of our students. In many ways, education is like magic: It is a process that, when done correctly, produces desired outcomes. Our task and challenge is to make the results of what we do in assessment knowable and known, to make educational outcomes predictable.

References

California State Commission for the Review of the Master Plan. *The Challenge of Change: A Reassessment of the California Community Colleges.* Sacramento: California State Commission for the Review of the Master Plan, 1986. 36 pp. (ED 269 048)

Commission for Educational Quality, Southern Regional Education Board. "Access to Quality Undergraduate Education." *Chronicle of Higher Education,* July 3, 1985, pp. 9–12.

Commission on Instruction, California Association of Community Colleges. *Mission, Finance, Accountability: A Framework for Improvement.* Sacramento: California Association of Community Colleges Press, 1984.

24

Education Commission of the States. "Transforming the State Role in Undergraduate Education: Time for a Different View." *The News, California Association of Community Colleges*, 1986, *32* (1), 4–9.

Joint Committee for the Review of the Master Plan for Higher Education, California Legislature. *California Community College Reform*. Sacramento: Joint Committee for the Review of the Master Plan for Higher Education, California Legislature, 1986.

Peters, T. J., and Waterman, R. H., Jr., *In Search of Excellence: Lessons from America's Best-Run Companies*. New York: Harper & Row, 1982.

Study Group on the Conditions of Excellence in American Higher Education. *Involvement in Learning: Realizing the Potential of American Higher Education*. Washington, D.C.: National Institute of Education, 1984.

Peter M. Hirsch is executive director of the California Association of Community Colleges.

Perhaps it is time to shift the focus of our attention from statewide mandated testing to classroom testing, surely a neglected area on most campuses.

Assessment and Improvement in Education

John Losak

Testing has taken on new dimensions as a part of higher education in the U.S. since several states began to legislate standards across the board for all students, not just those in specific professions (for example, law, nursing). At both the point of entry and the point of exit, testing programs have had an impact that is likely to increase in the near future, not to abate. Yet, by and large, classroom testing has been left untouched. One of the hidden factors driving the strong movement for minimal exit competencies is that classroom testing practices have not assured that students do indeed have basic skills.

A major assumption of both exit and entry-level testing is that any judgments that are arrived at can be sounder and perhaps even wiser if there are objective and standardized measures of achievement that can be reviewed. There is no question that the judgments will be arrived at with or without an exhaustive testing program. Rather, the question is whether those judgments can be improved by the use of a testing program. I believe that use of a standardized testing program either for course placement or for exit examinations can positively influence the judgments that are needed at these two points. Although knowledge of a student's high school curriculum is useful for initial course placement decisions, it is well known that the same subject is not taught with the same level of rigor or expectation in all high schools.

D. Bray, and M. J. Belcher (eds.). *Issues in Student Assessment.*
New Directions for Community Colleges, no. 59. San Francisco: Jossey-Bass, Fall 1987.

Therefore, a common placement examination helps the adviser or other decision maker who works with the student to effect a more appropriate placement than could be achieved if the student's achievement on the high school curriculum were the only basis for the decision making. The same analogy holds for decisions regarding the award of the associate degree to students who have progressed through two years of a college curriculum. Common testing has a way of assuring that common learning has occurred and of assuring the public and the legislators who represent the public that the goals, values, and objectives that have been deemed important and appropriate are in fact demonstrably achieved in an objective manner.

Is there then a direct link between the effort to improve the quality of education and the initiation of a program of standardized testing? A direct cause-and-effect relationship is quite difficult to establish. We in Florida have found that there are important spinoff effects that encourage the use of common examinations to make placement decisions and to assure minimal exit competencies. At Miami–Dade Community College, we have identified such spinoff effects as improved faculty morale, strong student support, and strong community support. All these effects reflect an increasingly positive attitude toward higher education. Moreover, there is evidence that student learning is affected by the level of expectations that instructors and others have of students and that, as these levels of expectations are raised on common examinations, student performance often follows.

It should also be said that the imposition of a standardized testing program on a shaky infrastructure probably does no more than reflect the weakness of the infrastructure. If the purpose of examination is to provide guidance on the strength or weakness of the curriculum, the testing program may be useful. However, the testing program will not in itself improve the quality of a poor infrastructure, although it may provide some guidance on the reforms that are needed in order for the curriculum and student learning to improve.

In summary, standardized testing for entry-level course placement decisions and exit examinations can be effective in assuring that certain basic concepts have been learned and that students who need remedial efforts receive the remedial courses. Moreover, there is evidence that the initiation of such a testing program conveys a message of positive educational value to many constituencies in higher education, including students, faculty, and lay citizens. We do well to remember that one of the real dangers of testing is to imply that all low-scoring students should be denied entrance to college. Studies that we at Miami–Dade Community College have conducted suggest that a student who is academically underprepared at entrance is not incapable of learning.

The exit test administered to sophomores in Florida can be cited as an example of state intervention in the examination process. The College-Level Academic Skills Test (CLAST) required by the state of Florida for an associate in arts degree consists of a series of tests designed to measure the communication and computation skills that community college and state university faculty members expect students who complete the sophomore year in college to possess.

In spring 1979, the Florida legislature enacted a law requiring identification of basic skills. In August 1979, the office that directs the program at the state level was established. During the next two years, these skills were identified, and item specifications were developed. The first test was given in fall 1982, and passing standards were first required in fall 1984.

It is difficult to estimate the overall cost in dollars of the CLAST to the state of Florida. At Miami–Dade Community College, we estimate that the direct costs are close to $7 per student. The state awards a contract to the office of instructional resources at the University of Florida, and the cost per student at the state level is approximately $13. If a 25 percent indirect cost is added to the local cost and the state cost, the $25 per-student cost multiplied by the 34,722 students tested in the 1985–86 academic year means that the total cost was $868,050.

One of the primary impacts of the intervention of state legislators in the assessment of students has been the clear message to faculty in the state of Florida that their past evaluations of students have not been satisfactory. The requirement that students demonstrate minimal scores before they are awarded an associate in arts degree continued to influence the award of grades by faculty. Test scores have risen during the four years in which the examination has been administered. We must be cautious in interpreting the higher scores, because there are at least three plausible explanations: The students who are taking the examination have gotten better, efforts to improve the curriculum have been successful, or wide dissemination of information about the form and content of the examination has made the students testwise. Another visible impact is that the number of associate in arts graduates has dropped. At Miami–Dade Community College, associate in arts graduates have been reduced by 40 percent.

CLAST is in place in the state of Florida essentially because the public had lost faith in the assessment process used by instructors in their classrooms to arrive at grades. Why is it that students who received the associate degree and who functioned at a C level or better in the classroom could not read, write, or compute at a high school level on the CLAST? The reason is that most instructors evaluate on a normative basis, and the talent that is before them decides the norm. In addition, few instructors have either the training or the inclination for the role of measurement and evaluation. A grade of C in an introductory psychology course at Swarthmore does not reflect the same mastery of content that the C grade does at a two-year open-door college. One important component of the issue of grade inflation is the fact that many instructors would have to award a very high proportion of F grades if the same expectations for content mastery were to be demanded at every institution, open-door community college as well as select liberal arts college.

As for the issue that the instructor must also be an evaluator, it is clear that American higher education does not prepare its graduates in discipline areas for the role of assessor. Some critics have argued that a master's degree or a Ph.D. in chemistry, history, geography, or English has not prepared the graduate either to instruct or to evaluate. I will focus here only on the fact that the instructor must spend between one quarter and one third of her or his time on measurement. I include in my estimate the time spent conceptualizing, developing, scoring, returning, and interpreting the materials to students. In all likelihood, few instructors in the disciplines just mentioned have had even a single course in measurement, much less advanced courses in assessment. Scriven (1982) offers a thorough and severe critique on this issue.

If I am right, the most viable solution is to weaken the link between the teaching and evaluation roles expected of instructors. This is not a new idea. As O'Neill (1987, p. 2) has noted, as early as 1869, Charles Eliot, the president of Harvard University, "called for an external examining body that would be distinct from the teaching body in the granting of degrees." At the University of Florida as recently as twenty years ago, university examiners prepared the tests for students in their first two years, and instructors had virtually no role in evaluation. This system was modeled after the system that Robert Hutchins had put into place at the University of Chicago.

In my opinion, the extreme dependence of our evaluation system on faculty judgment makes it an anachronism, and it should either be overhauled or discarded. Seventy-five or a hundred years ago, we could afford instructors' ineptness in assessment both because most students were highly selected and motivated to begin with and because classes were usually quite small, which increased the opportunity for the personal interaction that permits an instructor to make a relatively informed judgment about a student without having any real knowledge of assessment. In contrast, today's supermarket system of education, in which classes are very large, requires a different plan for the evaluation of student learning. Either faculty must become a great deal more sophisticated and rigorous in their system of evaluation, or evaluation by units external to the classroom will increase. Computer-assisted assessment may well be the technology that makes an increasingly rigorous and sophisticated student evaluation feasible. The institution where it is most important to separate teaching from evaluation activities is the two-year open-door college. However, because large numbers of the students who enroll in classes at any college are underprepared, the question of the extent to which teaching and evaluation can appropriately be made more separate than they currently are is germane to all institutions of higher education.

Finally, if the role of the instructor as evaluator decreases, will standards be imposed from without? It is precisely the inability of those within higher education to solve the assessment issue that leads legislative bodies to impose standards and procedures. Increasing our reliance on common examinations written by local discipline experts—that is, departmental and even baccalaureate-level examinations, which some colleges still provide—will serve to provide benchmarks; relieve the instructor from time-consuming, frustrating, and often onerous tasks; and permit the instructor to focus on the teaching function. It should also provide a more realistic basis for the appraisal of student learning.

Perhaps it is time to shift the focus of our attention away from statewide mandated testing to classroom testing, as I have suggested here. It is in the classroom that student learning is most directly assessed, and it is in the classroom that thought and energy should be devoted to our attempts to improve higher education through assessment.

References

O'Neill, J. P. *The Political Economy of Assessment: Research and Development Update.* New York: College Board, 1987.
Scriven, M. "Professorial Ethics." *Journal of Higher Education,* 1982, *53* (3), 307–317.

John Losak is dean of institutional research at Miami–Dade Community College in Miami, Florida.

Gains in learning are expected of college students. This chapter reviews the pros and cons of value-added assessment and proposes several alternative approaches.

Value-Added Assessment: College Education and Student Growth

Marcia J. Belcher

Higher education is under fire. Officials in the federal government warn of closer scrutiny. State legislators move to assess the impact of state dollars on higher education. Major groups have issued reports that decry the quality of undergraduate education and urge reforms. At the heart of these matters are the questions of what is excellence in higher education and how it can best be attained.

Astin (1985) argues that the traditional views of excellence, which are tied to reputation (translated as selectivity and size) and resources (also tied to reputation), do not really either measure or promote excellence in higher education. To replace them, Astin proposes an approach that emphasizes educational impact or value added, since "true excellence resides in the ability of the college or university to affect its students favorably, to enhance their intellectual development, and to make a positive difference in their lives" (Astin, 1984, p. 27).

The value-added approach emphasized by Astin focuses on changes in students between the beginning and the end of their college careers. As Turnbull (1987, p. 3) has noted, "the root idea of assessing how much students learn or improve or grow in school or in college, as well as how they

D. Bray, and M. J. Belcher (eds.). *Issues in Student Assessment.*
New Directions for Community Colleges, no. 59. San Francisco: Jossey-Bass, Fall 1987.

stand at graduation, is not only a good and important idea but obviously one that lies near the heart of the education enterprise."

It is an idea that is gaining momentum. State coordinating boards in Tennessee and South Dakota require value-added testing and several other states, including Colorado, Maryland, New Jersey, and Virginia, are considering the approach. An increasing number of individual institutions have implemented value-added initiatives. The best-known example is Northeast Missouri State University, which has used such a system since 1974. Its approach includes using standardized tests for freshmen and sophomores, major field examinations for graduating students, and attitude surveys of students and alumni.

Arguments for and Against Value-Added Assessment

In the current debates over value-added assessment, three major issues keep emerging. One issue focuses on growth and on whether this is the best way of conceptualizing excellence in higher education. The second issue is how the installation of value-added assessment will change the institution. The third issue is whether the value-added measurement method can capture the learning process in higher education.

Value-Added Assessment Emphasizes Growth. Should growth or competence be the standard used to judge excellence? To base our judgment of an institution on the quality of its graduates ignores the skills and abilities with which its graduates arrived. A selective college can be confident that its graduates will be successful, since its students have been selected on these very same measures. Including the inputs could change the institutions that are considered excellent.

Astin (1984) argues that value-added assessment promotes the goal of educational equity, since it places the emphasis on improvement. Students are not denied opportunities because they perform at a low level on entry. Gains or improvements are the focal point, and institutions and individuals alike have an opportunity to be excellent under this approach.

For others, improvement is an insufficient basis for the making of judgments. These people argue for bottom-line ("minimal") standards that all must meet and discount the issue of improvement. While Manning (1987, p. 52) agrees that value-added assessment is a good method for evaluating instructional programs, he worries that the "truly deceptive aspect of the value-added philosophy lies in the effort of some of its proponents to tie student assessment too narrowly to the notion of improvement rather than to criteria of competency." Most proponents of value-added assessment hasten to note that measuring improvement does not replace the possibility of setting a floor by exit standards.

Exit standards are often thought of as involving assessment at the time when a student is ready to receive a degree. Catanzaro (1987) points to the diversity of students within the community college system and to their broad spectrum of goals. He argues that many attend community colleges specifically because they want a value-added education (that is, specific skills or competencies), not a set of competencies tied to the completion of a degree.

Even if all were to agree that it is important to measure improvement, it can be difficult to do so. Measurement specialists have wrestled for years with ways of measuring and comparing gains. Another problem lies in linking growth to instruction. As Warren (1984) notes, it may be that students are of such high ability that they will learn a great deal, whatever the quality of the instruction that is provided. Also, high entering skill levels that provide little room for growth may limit the amount of change that is seen.

Another measurement issue involves the question of whether the same students are being measured at the beginning and at the end. Looking at the average increase in a measure taken at entrance and graduation may say more about the retention policy of the institution than it does about the quality of the education that the institution provides (Turnbull, 1987). If the only students who are left are the students who entered scoring high, then improvement is automatically shown.

Value-Added Assessment Will Change the Way in Which Institutions Operate. Critics of value-added assessment fear that value-added testing on a statewide basis will lead to a uniform curriculum and hamper individuality. Teachers may feel forced to emphasize skills assessed by the test to the detriment of other subject areas.

Astin and Ewell (1985) argue that colleges and universities are in the business of developing student learning. A value-added perspective asks faculty to state objectives for the curriculum and to think in developmental terms. If the result is that faculty become more explicit about what should be taught to all students and more attentive to whether learning occurs, then a uniform curriculum is a benefit, not a drawback. The process would help to focus institutional attention directly on the teaching-learning process.

Value-Added Assessment Makes Assumptions About What Learning Is. Can value-added assessment capture the process of learning? Arguing that learning in higher education involves a reconfiguring of patterns, Manning (1987, p. 52) concludes that "a valid measure of initial status in a subject matter may be inappropriate to measure performance at a higher level of learning." Turnbull (1987, p. 4) agrees, stating that it is "the patterns and interrelations among the indicators that count." Warren (1984) follows a different line of reasoning to reach a similar conclusion. He argues that an effective pretest for a course assesses the prerequisite knowledge needed for the course but that this knowledge is not the knowledge or capability needed at the end of the course. Nevertheless, using a different test at the end of the course would make it impossible to compare scores. Warren believes that the same argument holds true when we try to compare institutions.

Astin and Ewell (1985) reply that in many areas knowledge is cumulative, hierarchical, and measurable along a continuum. Therefore, knowledge is amenable to value-added assessment. Even critics of value-added assessment concede that it can be useful when it comes to knowing more about generic competencies, such as writing and critical thinking.

Warren (1984) believes that much value-added measurement is trivial and cites pre- and posttesting of course content as an example. He argues that performance at the end of a course is an acceptable indicator of the effects of the course. Astin and Ewell (1985) reply that value-added assessment in courses is only one component of the value added and that the implementation of value-added assessment has not trivialized discussions of learning outcomes at institutions where it has been tried.

Although critics of value-added assessment have been assured that it does not need to be confined to the use of a standardized test, the impression continues. For example, Turnbull (1987, p. 5) urges that a variety of assessment techniques be used to measure student progress, adding that "the idea that a test is going to give you more than a fraction of what you are interested in learning about progress toward the broad goals of higher education is, at this date, totally illusory."

Alternative Methods of Measuring the Value Added

Though value-added assessment has traditionally been thought of as pre- and posttesting, that approach is not the only way in which value-added assessment can be implemented. According to Turnbull (1987), both progress and the end product are important in assessing the value of education. Assessing improvement is most useful when we compare the effectiveness of institutions or programs from year to year. He suggests preserving a set of senior theses as benchmarks for varying levels of acceptability and recording the proportion of the senior class that meets the various benchmarks. The benchmarks can be saved and used to compare individual institutions with one another as well.

The beauty of the approach just described is that it allows the evaluation to be more holistic than it can be in standardized testing. However, the approach has several drawbacks, including deciding on what will be assessed (for example, creativity, grammar, critical thinking, logical presentation of ideas) and on how to assess it reliably.

If standardized tests and placement tests are used and if improvement in writing and math skills is the issue (as it is in many community colleges), then a second and perhaps supplemental process might be employed to assess the value added. I propose a four-step process whereby the institution would administer an entry-level test in basic skills and use the resulting scores to place students in their initial level of coursework; decide which curricular variables should be related to the level of basic skills measured at the point when the student graduates and collect information on these skills for each student; select a test of basic skills to be given at the point of graduation (it can be the test used at entry, or it can be a more difficult test on the same content area); and conduct a yearly analysis (using a statistical technique, such as multiple regression) to assess the extent to which the entering level of basic skills and the curricular variables predict the exit level of basic skills.

Such a process could answer the question about the relative contributions of entering skills and the curriculum. Because the analysis would account for the possibility of shifting levels of basic skills, the changing contributions of the curriculum across the years could be assessed.

Results from the type of analysis just described showed that the curriculum at Miami-Dade Community College played a large role in predictions of exit skills in computation for A.A. graduates but that reading skills still depended heavily on the level of reading ability that students brought to college (Belcher, 1986). In computation, the entering level of basic skills was less predictive for black students than it was for other groups. No differences were found in communication. Figure 1 depicts the results for communication, and Figure 2 depicts the results for computation.

The analysis just described used the Comparative Guidance and Placement Program (CGP) tests in reading, writing, and computation to measure entry-level skills. The four subtests of the College-Level Academic Skills Test (CLAST)—reading, writing, computation, and a holistically scored essay—were used to measure exit-level skills. The curricular variables were grades in two English courses and one math course and the number of credits earned in developmental English, math, and English-as-a-second-language courses. The amount of time that had elapsed since the students completed their major English and math courses was included to account for the forgetting that can take place over time. Belcher (1986) provides further details on the study.

This approach to value-added assessment has some statistical and conceptual problems. For example, it assumes both that the curriculum can be defined and that the effects are cumulative and linear. The relationship between the curriculum and the exit level of skills depends in part on the strength of the relationship between entry and exit skills. In the instance just described, the exact amount of change in skill level could not be assessed.

However, the inherent relativity of this approach can also be viewed as a strength. The question, What is the value of a college education? must be countered by the question, Compared to what? While the ultimate answer might compare the skill development of college graduates with the skill development of students who do not graduate (since students can continue to mature whether they are in college or not), this approach assumes that,

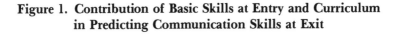

Figure 1. Contribution of Basic Skills at Entry and Curriculum in Predicting Communication Skills at Exit

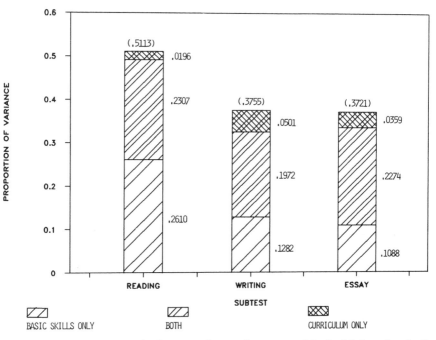

without the college curriculum, students who enter with the highest level of basic skills will exit with the highest levels and that those who enter at the bottom will exit at the bottom. If the curriculum helped to maintain these rankings, then differences due only to the curriculum would not be seen. It could also be argued that the impact of curriculum could be unidirectional; that is, curriculum affects only those at the bottom, not those at the top. Therefore, improvement would be demonstrated statistically, but important differences would be masked by this level of analysis.

Conclusion

Value-added assessment is one of several solutions currently being offered as tools for remediating the weaknesses of higher education. It will be some time before sufficient evidence is available to judge the effectiveness of this approach and to determine whether proponents or critics were correct in their evaluations. Legislators and the general public need an approach that is both valid and simple. If value-added assessment is implemented without regard to the information needs of administrators, faculty, and students or to the unique character of the institution, it will probably fail. If

Figure 2. Contribution of Basic Skills at Entry and Curriculum in Predicting Computation Skills at Exit

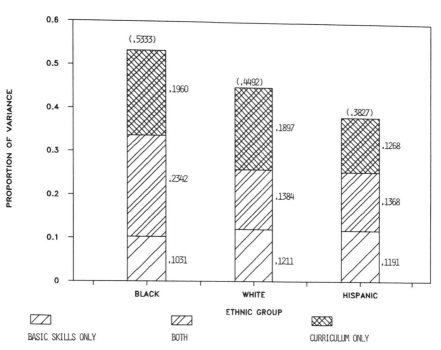

it is implemented thoughtfully with the full participation of all interested parties and with multiple measures and approaches, it may succeed in providing focus to the real goal of higher education—teaching and learning—and in bringing lasting and beneficial change to higher education.

References

Astin, A. W. "Excellence and Equity: Achievable Goals for American Education." *Phi Kappa Phi Journal*, 1984, *64* (2), 24–29.

Astin, A. W. *Achieving Educational Excellence: A Critical Assessment of Priorities and Practices in Higher Education.* San Francisco: Jossey-Bass, 1985.

Astin, A. W., and Ewell, P. T. "The Value-Added Debate . . . Continued." *American Association for Higher Education Bulletin*, 1985, *37* (8), 11–13.

Belcher, M. J. "Predicting Competence in Basic Skills After Two Years of College: The Roles of Entering Basic Skills and the Curriculum." Paper presented at the annual meeting of the American Educational Research Association, San Francisco, April 16–20, 1986. 28 pp. (ED 270 136)

Catanzaro, J. L. "Counterpoint." *Community, Technical, and Junior College Journal*, 1987, *57* (4), 53.

Manning, W. H. "Point." *Community, Technical, and Junior College Journal*, 1987, *57* (4), 52.

38

Turnbull, W. W. "Can 'Value Added' Add Value to Education?" *Research and Development Update,* Jan. 1987, p. 3-5.

Warren, J. "The Blind Alley of Value Added." *American Association for Higher Education Bulletin,* 1984, *37* (1), 10-13.

Marcia J. Belcher is senior research associate at Miami–Dade Community College in Miami, Florida.

Teacher-made tests are more than assessment devices: They are a fundamental part of the educational process. They can define instructional purposes, influence what students study, and help instructors to gain perspective on their courses. How well the tests accomplish these purposes is a function of their quality.

The Role of the Teacher-Made Test in Higher Education

Scarvia B. Anderson

Let us examine two myths. *Myth one: Students study because they want to learn.* A few students study because of their intrinsic interest in the subject matter—accounting, personality theory, the English novel. But, most undergraduates study only as much as they have to—to get by and to get through, to retain their scholarships or to maintain their athletic eligibility, to keep their families or their employers off their backs. *Myth two: Colleges and universities have a profound influence on students' ability and motivation to learn.* There are a few notable exceptions, but by and large the more knowledgeable and able students in high school are also the more knowledgeable and able students in college. Furthermore, the students who are more knowledgeable and able to start with are the students who are likely to profit from instruction. Thus, when colleges are compared on the basis of output, the variance between institutions can be attributed more to the characteristics of the students whom the institutions admit than it can to the programs offered. The value-added approach to institutional evaluation keeps selective colleges from taking credit where it is not due, but any comparisons between the value added by different colleges must take into account the caliber of the students that each college had to work with.

D. Bray, and M. J. Belcher (eds.). *Issues in Student Assessment.*
New Directions for Community Colleges, no. 59. San Francisco: Jossey-Bass, Fall 1987.

The editors of the *New York Times* headlined an article I wrote about classroom tests "Tests That Stand the Test of Time" (Anderson, 1985). After it appeared, I received many letters from college professors, school administrators, and others saying that it was about time someone had something to say about something other than standardized tests. But, one writer took me firmly to task for denigrating standardized tests. That was not my point at all; the two kinds of tests serve quite different purposes. I emphasized that standardized tests, the ones that get all the publicity, frequently have something to do with who gets certain educational opportunities, while teacher-made tests, the silent majority that you do not hear much about, are the tests that determine what education is.

Long before standardized testing became a multimillion-dollar business, students at every educational level took the local tests and examinations that determined whether they got an A or a C, passed the course, accumulated enough credits to receive a degree, or received a favorable recommendation from the instructor. Such tests have three fundamental educational properties: First, more than any other educational device, teacher-made tests tell students what the purpose of the instruction is and what is expected of them. If the English professor asks only one question on *Moby Dick* and it is, What different kinds of whales did they encounter on their voyage? he has certainly given students an inadequate reason for studying this great novel. Second, what students study is what they think they are going to be asked about in the instructor's tests. The first myth was that students study for the joy of learning. The student below the graduate level who does is rare indeed, and some professors complain that many graduate students are not self-motivated. There is no point in Xeroxing supplementary reading lists if students are not queried on the contents of the readings. Third, the preparation of good tests helps instructors to gain perspective on their courses and sometimes even to understand better what they are teaching. Paul Diederich, a distinguished English teacher and scholar, was once asked if he understood Eliot's *Four Quartets*. He scratched his head and said, "I don't know. I've never tried to write an exercise on it."

Knowing that tests and examinations define instructional purposes and instructors' expectations, profoundly influence what students study, and help instructors to gain perspective on their courses places considerable responsibility on those who make up the tests. People who develop standardized tests for commercial establishments have the luxury of plying their trade full-time. College professors have to fit test making into a schedule that includes a great many other things: preparation and delivery of courses, committee or administrative assignments, student advising, research, and so on. It is no wonder that many of the tests that are made up hurriedly on the way to class, that are kept in the files of student clubs, or that are stored in the microcomputers that departments are so proud of are not very good tests. They do not focus on what is most important, they do not inspire students to study what is worth studying, and they do not present an intellectual challenge to the examinees, not to mention the examiner.

There are basically two functions that educational tests should assess: knowledge and skills. Knowledge, which includes understanding and inference as well as information, can be measured both by good essay questions and by short-answer, multiple-choice, and other objective types of items. Even the much-maligned true-false questions can be used if the task is in fact to identify the truth or falsity of propositions. For example, these seem to be legitimate true-false items (Ebel, 1965, p. 139):

> A receiver in bankruptcy acquires title to the bankrupt's
> property.   T F
>
> More heat energy is required to warm a gallon of cool water
> from 50 degrees F to 80 degrees F than to heat a pint of the
> same cool water to boiling point.   T F

The shortcut of statements taken verbatim from the textbook neither puts the true-false item to good use nor produces a good test.

Of all the objective types of items, the multiple-choice form is probably the most generally useful, and, contrary to popular opinion, multiple-choice items can be used to measure a diversity of cognitive processes. For example, consider these items:

> The concept of the plasma membrane as a simple sievelike structure
> is inadequate to explain the
> a. passage of gases involved in respiration into and out of the cell.
> b. passage of simple organic molecules, such as glucose, into the
>   cell.
> c. failure of protein molecules to pass through the membrane.
> d. ability of the cell to admit selectively some inorganic ions while
>   excluding others.

To select the correct answer (d), the student must know that the living plasma membrane has properties in addition to those served by the thin films usually used in laboratory demonstrations of osmosis (Educational Testing Service, 1963).

> *Thick with towns and hamlets studded, and with streams*
> *and vapors gray,*
> *Like a shield embossed with silver, round and vast the landscape lay.*
>
> *At my feet the city slumbered. From its chimneys, here and there*
> *Wreaths of snow-white smoke, ascending, vanished ghost-like*
> *into air.*

The poet most likely to have written these lines is
a. Stephen Vincent Benet
b. Emily Dickinson
c. Henry Wadsworth Longfellow
d. Edgar Allan Poe
e. Walt Whitman

Note that in this item the student is not asked or expected to recognize the lines from memory. Instead, he or she is expected to identify them with the style of one of the poets (Longfellow) or, conversely, to reject them as unlike the style of any of the other four.

It is far from easy to write good multiple-choice items. Even the best item writers are frequently frustrated in their attempts to invent a plausible but incorrect fourth or fifth choice, and some materials do not lend themselves to a fixed number of choices.

Harold Gulliksen, the well-known measurement theorist, advocates a type of item that combines multiple choice with matching. These items are easier and quicker to construct than either of the parent types, and they are quite well suited to certain kinds of content. Each exercise presents a small number of responses and a large number of "statements" (terms, phrases, quotations, and so on), and students use each response several times. For example, in current history, you might list five religions and ask students to characterize each of fifteen nations in terms of the religion of the majority:

Religion of Majority: a. Catholic; b. Hindu; c. Moslem; d. Protestant; e. Other

___ 1. Argentina	___ 6. Japan	___ 11. U.S.S.R.
___ 2. Canada	___ 7. Malaysia	___ 12. U.K.
___ 3. Costa Rica	___ 8. Pakistan	___ 13. Uruguay
___ 4. France	___ 9. Philippines	___ 14. U.S.
___ 5. India	___ 10. Republic of Ireland	___ 15. Yemen

You can see the possibilities of this type of item, which is sometimes called a *key-list exercise*, for genres or periods in literature, types of government, classes of compounds in chemistry, concepts in business law, and so on.

By definition, college professors profess on many topics, and many of them profess to despise objective tests. If they admit using them, it is only out of practical necessity with their largest classes. However, I hope to have shown that objective tests can do a rather nice job of measurement in many instances and that a set of good objective questions is superior to a set of bad essay questions. By *bad* I mean questions like these:

Discuss the causes of the Civil War.
What is the greatest social achievement of the twentieth century?

The responses to such questions are almost impossible to grade fairly. The best grades usually go to the more verbal students, not to the students who know more about the subject matter. Of course, instructors who write good essay questions have clear grading rubrics in mind from the outset.

There are circumstances in which instructors must ask students to write their answers—for example, when they want to know how well they can write, whether they wish only to observe the students' mastery of simple mechanical conventions or their ability to express complex ideas or write creatively.

As I indicated earlier, there are two things that college tests should assess, knowledge and skills, and the reason is simple: Knowledge and skills are what most college courses are all about. Up to this point (with the exception of the issue of writing tests), I have focused on the measurement of knowledge. To measure skills, you usually need to ask students to do something:

Make a scale drawing of a public building.
Speak extemporaneously on a popular topic.
Write a letter of application for a job.
Prepare a soufflé.
Write a proposal for an experiment.
Analyze a blood sample.
Transpose a piece of music into another key.
Edit a technical manuscript.
Write a computer program.

It is seldom sufficient to ask students about drawing, speaking, writing, cooking, and so on, although there is usually some basic knowledge important to the development of such skills that can be measured separately.

The guidelines for the construction of good performance tests do not differ from the guidelines for the construction of good paper-and-pencil tests of knowledge: First, specify the criteria to be used for rating or scoring the performance or product. Second, state the problem so that students are absolutely clear about what they are supposed to do. Third, if possible, tell students the basis on which their performance will be judged. Fourth, avoid any irrelevant difficulties in the content or procedures of testing. For example, do not require students to work through an elaborate set of written instructions in order to demonstrate that they can carry out routine computations. Fifth, if possible, give the students a chance to perform the task more than once or to perform several task samples.

Most colleges and universities make an attempt to judge the teaching proficiency of faculty members. While many of these attempts are informal, some departments are seeking more systematic ways of rating teaching proficiency in terms of such variables as course content and organization, classroom techniques, encouragement of students to think creatively, and evaluation practices. Review of some of the instructor's tests is essential in order to rate him or her on evaluation practices. However, review of the faculty member's tests and examinations may also shed light on other variables. For example, if examination questions are limited to textbook examples, there is little evidence that the faculty member encourages students to think creatively. Thus, the examinations that are used to evaluate students may also figure in the evaluation of teaching proficiency.

Those who develop and administer aptitude, basic skills, IQ, and other standardized tests are constantly being called on to defend the use of such tests. The tests discriminate against some segment of the population, the tests are "coachable," the tests exert an unhealthy influence on the curriculum—these are just some of the charges. But, how many college teachers have ever had to defend the fact of course examinations and quizzes? Students expect them, administrators expect them, regents expect them. What college teachers should be called on to defend is the quality of the tests that they give and the influence that the tests exert on student learning.

References

Anderson, S. B. "Tests That Stand the Test of Time." *New York Times,* August 18, 1985, Section 12, p. 61.

Ebel, R. L. *Measuring Educational Achievement.* Englewood Cliffs, N.J.: Prentice-Hall, 1965.

Educational Testing Service. *Multiple-Choice Questions: A Close Look.* Princeton, N.J.: Educational Testing Service, 1963.

Scarvia B. Anderson is an independent consultant on human assessment and program evaluation, adjunct professor of psychology at Georgia Institute of Technology, and former senior vice-president of Educational Testing Service.

The use of direct writing assessment on a large scale seems to be growing. This chapter reviews the process of developing a writing assessment program.

Assessment of Writing Skills Through Essay Tests

Linda Crocker

The essay is the oldest form of written examination. Dubois (1970) has documented its use in Chinese civil service tests as long ago as 2200 B.C. Written essay examinations were used in medieval European universities. In the nineteenth century, Francis Galton (1948) used the marks assigned by Cambridge University examiners to an eight-day essay examination to demonstrate that achievement test scores for large samples followed an approximately normal distribution. Even the first British civil service examinations were entirely essay in format. In the United States, the essay item was the predominant form used in college admissions testing until the 1920s, when the more easily and more objectively scored multiple-choice item became popular (Breland, 1983).

While widespread use of items requiring written responses has waned in the measurement of many academic subjects, essay testing continues to play a dominant role in the measurement of writing ability. Thus, the measurement literature distinguishes between the notions of essay compositions and essay test items. In essay subject area examinations, knowledge of a specific academic subject, such as history or biological science, is assessed. The examinee's writing ability is usually considered to be peripheral to the characteristic of major interest. In the essay composition, the examinee's writing ability is the trait being assessed. The written essay represents a

D. Bray, and M. J. Belcher (eds.). *Issues in Student Assessment.*
New Directions for Community Colleges, no. 59. San Francisco: Jossey-Bass, Fall 1987.

performance sample that allows for direct assessment of the examinee's writing ability. The focus of this chapter is on the use of the essay for direct assessment of writing ability.

Why Should Essay Examinations Be Used?

The use of essay items to test examinees' knowledge of the rules of grammar, knowledge of the mechanics of writing, or spelling ability is not generally recommended. These skills can be tested more efficiently with objective test item formats. Nevertheless, the essay is still widely used to test ability to organize information, express ideas, generate original thought or solutions, communicate with expression, or demonstrate stylistic aspects of writing. The essay format has some well-known limitations, including the time-consuming scoring process and the subjectivity involved in the evaluation of examinee's responses. Despite these problems, the credibility that essay items have with instructors, administrators, examinees, and the public at large (Rentz, 1984) is a strong argument for their continued use. In this same vein, Diederich (1974, p. 1) pointed out the logical appeal of collecting writing samples when we want to draw inferences about students' writing abilities: "Whenever we want to find out whether young people can swim, we have them jump into a pool and swim."

Today, the use of direct writing assessment on a large scale seems to be growing. Direct writing assessment is included in the National Assessment of Educational Progress, the English composition test administered as part of the College Board's admissions testing program, the Test of English as a Foreign Language (TOEFL), statewide assessment programs for public school students, and most recently statewide assessment programs at the college and university level. A prominent example of the last type of program is the state of Florida's College-Level Academic Skills Test (CLAST).

The purpose of the writing assessment programs just named are quite diverse. They range from differentiating among examinees for selection, to certification of minimal competency skills, to identification of individual strengths or weaknesses for instructional placement or remediation. Thus, the first step in the development of a writing assessment must be to identify the primary purpose to be served by the data that will be collected. Adhering to the goals of the assessment is essential in subsequent decisions about how to structure the writing assessment program.

Once the objectives to be sampled by the writing tasks have been specified, the process of instituting a large-scale testing program for the direct assessment of writing typically involves a series of steps, such as those outlined by Meredith and Williams (1984) or Quellmalz (1984b). These steps include the development and field-testing of a large pool of suitable topics or prompts, the development of scoring procedures, the selection and training of scorers, the administration of the examination, the scoring of the resulting writing samples, and the assessment of the reliability and validity of the examinees' scores. These steps will be considered in the remainder of this chapter.

Developing Prompts

An important consideration in large-scale writing assessment is the development of a sizable pool of topics or prompts that can be used to generate the examinees' written responses. Unlike objective tests, which can be kept secure after development and reused many times, new topics must be available each time the writing examination is administered, because examinees can remember the essay topics and pass them on to cohorts who will take the test at a later sitting. In creating multiple prompts, the task is to ensure that the topics are different enough to offer no advantage to those who write at later sittings yet similar enough to maintain comparability in terms of the skills assessed and the level of difficulty.

In assessments of basic writing skills, the prompt typically specifies the topic, the audience to whom the writing is to be addressed, a suggested structure for the response, and the mode of discourse (Quellmalz, 1984b; Meredith and Williams, 1984). Mode of discourse (or aim of writing) is illustrated by the five categories suggested by the National Council of Teachers of English: narrating, explaining, describing, reporting, and persuading (Tate and others, 1979). In writing assessment programs in higher education, the intended audience and the mode of discourse are sometimes implied rather than explicitly stated in the prompt.

Most authorities recommend that an essay prompt should have seven characteristics: First, the topic should be a thought-provoking stimulus that gives the examinee some latitude for self-expression. Second, the topic should be specific enough to ensure some common theme or core of content in the responses of examinees, although their viewpoints may vary. Third, the prompt should provide a structure for the examinee's response. This structure can often be achieved by suggesting that the examinee use examples, give an opinion and supporting reasons, or address both sides of an issue. Fourth, the content of the topic should be within the general experience of all examinees. For example, an item that asks examinees to describe their position on a particular recent event may leave some examinees at a disadvantage because they are uninformed in this area. Fifth, the topics should not afford an advantage to examinees of a particular gender, racial or cultural group, or socioeconomic class. For example, a topic related to sports can be viewed as biased against females. Even such a topic as "My Most Memorable Summer Vacation" may leave some examinees with little to write if they have never had an opportunity to take a summer vacation. Sixth, the topic should avoid controversial political or social issues. Asking examinees to state their positions on abortion or use of illegal drugs may introduce an unwanted bias into the scoring process, since some raters might find it difficult to evaluate objectively papers that expressed positions drastically at odds with their own personal beliefs. Seventh, expectations for the length of the essay and scoring criteria should be explicitly stated. Time limits should also be specified.

One fairly controversial issue in the development of writing prompts that must be addressed is whether to provide examinees with a choice among several topics or to require all examinees to write on the same topic. The proponents of multiple topics argue that examinees usually perceive this practice as fairer and that it may be a way of avoiding undesirable cultural bias in the selection of topics. The critics of providing a choice of topics cite the difficulty of ensuring that the topics are equal in difficulty and the possibility that examinees who unwittingly choose the more difficult topic may earn lower scores (Hoetker, 1982; Rosenbaum, 1985). Another problem is that examinees who begin to write on one topic and then change their minds lose valuable time. At present, no single position is universally accepted in large-scale writing assessment programs for secondary school and college students, but Dovell and Buhr (1986) point out that the literature on the reliability of essay scores generally advocates requiring all examinees to write on the same topic or topics.

After the prompts are written, they are typically reviewed by a panel of experts who check to see that they are consistent with the purpose of the assessment program. The experts may also evaluate other qualities of the prompts, such as those mentioned earlier. Technical aspects of the prompts, such as grammar, readability, length, and the quality of any artwork, should also be reviewed.

Developing Scoring Procedures

The three most commonly used scoring procedures in large-scale writing assessments are holistic scoring, analytic scoring, and primary trait scoring. The term *holistic scoring* refers to the practice of having a rater read the essay and make an overall judgment about its quality. Typically, a number from a continuum is assigned as the outcome of this scoring process. The rater is usually provided with some verbal description of the qualities that should be considered in assigning ratings. The rater may also be provided with criteria for assigning each separate numeric value. Sample responses that typify each category in the scoring continuum are sometimes provided as reference points.

The terms *analytic scoring* refers to the practice of having the rater evaluate each essay with a specific list of features or points in mind and assign a separate score for each point. The total score assigned to the response is the sum of the scores for the specific features. The best-known example of an analytic score guide for essay compositions is probably Diederich's (1974) scale, which requires the scoring of ideas, organization, wording, flavor, usage, punctuation, spelling, and handwriting. The rating guide for functional writing used in the Illinois writing assessment program rates examinees' essays on a six-point scale for focus, support, organization, and mechanics (Chapman, Fyans, and Kerins, 1984).

The term *primary trait scoring* refers to procedures developed for use in scoring the writing samples collected as part of the National Assessment of Educational Progress (NAEP) (Lloyd-Jones, 1977). Primary trait scoring is based on the assumption that the purpose of assessment is to determine the ability of examinees to perform fairly specific types of writing tasks. In the context of a task involving writing a letter to persuade a reluctant landlord to allow the writer to keep a puppy, Mullis (1984) describes the four scoring categories for the evaluation of the resulting writing as follows: "Generally a '1' paper would present little or no evidence, a '2' would have few or inappropriate reasons, a '3' would be well thought out with several appropriate reasons, and a '4' would be well organized with reasons supported by compelling details." In contrast to holistic and analytic scoring, primary trait scoring uses scoring criteria that vary with the task assigned.

Training Raters

Mullis (1984) has described the procedures used by the Educational Testing Service for scoring the English composition test and the NAEP writing exercises. In general, a set of anchor papers that a panel of expert or master raters has scored are selected to represent each scoring category. Training includes the discussion of scoring guidelines and the particular features of each category, illustrations using the anchor or standard papers. Meredith and Williams (1984) advocate the use of papers that represent both solid and borderline examples of the scoring categories. During training, raters receive feedback on the extent to which their ratings match those of the experts.

After training, raters must demonstrate their expertise by successfully rating a set of qualifying papers that a panel of experts or master scorers has already rated. It is necessary to establish a criterion for satisfactory performance on this qualifying task in advance. Sachse (1984) reports that trainees in the Texas writing assessment program must match master scorers' ratings on at least 75 percent of two sets of qualifying papers before they can serve as scorers.

Field-Testing the Prompts and Scoring System

After review, the prompts are field-tested by administering them to a sample of respondents on an experimental basis. Responses obtained in the field tests are scored. Sachse (1984) suggests that the field test responses should be examined for possible miscues in the prompt, the possibility of reader boredom, the ease with which the scoring guides can be applied, the appeal to examinees, and the level of difficulty. Topics must be equal in difficulty if examinees are to be given a choice of topics in the actual writing situation or if examinees must score above a fixed performance standard and different topics are to be used on different testing occasions. The most common practice for estimating the difficulty level of a prompt is to compute the mean score of the responses to it (Dovell and Buhr, 1986). It is also desirable to examine the variance of the distribution of the responses to the prompts that have been field-tested. Rosenbaum (1985) describes some technical approaches to the scaling of topics for difficulty.

From the field test it is also possible to estimate the time required to score a typical essay and hence to estimate the number of raters who will be needed, the amount of time required to complete the scoring, and the cost of scoring. It is also possible to identify any additional issues that may need to be addressed in the training of raters.

Scoring the Writing Samples

When a large-scale writing assessment has produced thousands of essays, such details as the physical setting for the raters' workplace and the logistics of arranging the essays into packets and distributing them to raters become crucial. One common practice is to assign raters to small groups presided over by a table leader who is responsible for supervising the scoring process within that group. In addition, there are usually one or more chief raters who are available as resource persons to answer questions that may arise. Ideally, each rater should record scores on a separate sheet that other raters will not see.

Typically, each essay is read by two or more raters, and the scores that they award are combined by summing or averaging in order to determine the examinee's final score. A critical part of most scoring processes is how to deal with the cases when the scores assigned to an essay do not agree. In a minimum competency testing situation, adjudication of such cases is necessary only when the discrepant ratings fall on opposite sides of the pass cut score. In norm-referenced writing assessments, adjudication can be invoked when the discrepancies exceed a certain range of points. Breland (1983) notes that one fairly common procedure for adjudication is to have another reader (for example, the table leader or chief reader) score the essays that have received discrepant ratings.

Once the actual scoring process is under way, a common practice is to add some blind, prescored standard papers to the responses so that the accuracy of the scorers can be monitored and drift in scoring standards can be controlled. Frequent practice calibration sessions should also be conducted during the scoring process to maintain rater consistency. For example,

Meredith and Williams (1984) describe a process in which each day's scoring session begins with a recalibration round using a standard set of five to ten papers.

Assessing Reliability

When the term *reliability* is applied to test scores, it generally means the degree of consistency in relative scores earned by a given group of examinees over replicated testing situations. In large-scale writing assessments, where different packets of papers must be graded by different scorers, the issue of reliability usually centers on whether different raters would assign similar ratings to the same composition. Another question is whether the performance of examinees is consistent over different topics within the same mode and over different modes of writing. As noted earlier, one important step in the planning of large-scale writing assessment is to conduct field tests of the prompts and scoring procedures. The data from these field tests should be collected within the framework of a research design that allows these reliability issues to be investigated. After the assessment system is in place, ongoing monitoring of the reliability of the scoring process should be part of the assessment program.

A variety of approaches can be used to demonstrate the degree of reliability in the scores assigned to writing samples. Three are commonly used: indexes of decision consistency, such as the proportion of examinees consistently classified into pass/fail categories or the proportion of examinees consistently classified into all categories used in the scoring system; correlations of the scores assigned by all possible pairs of raters or correlations of the scores obtained from the same individuals on different writing samples; and variance components and generalizability coefficients obtained by applying analysis of variance. From a technical standpoint, the analysis of variance procedures, which are based on generalizability theory, are generally recommended by measurement experts (Coffman, 1971; Meredith and Williams, 1984). There are two main reasons for this recommendation: The approach can be applied for any number of raters, and it makes it possible to estimate how many different sources of variance (for example, raters, tasks, occasions, time limits, instructions to raters or examinees) affect the scores of a set of essays. Crocker and Algina (1986) show how generalizability theory can be used in various single-facet designs where multiple raters rate essays. Llabre (1978) provides a detailed illustration of the application of generalizability theory to writing assessment, using raters, modes of writing, and occasions as sources of variation.

It is important for the method that is used to estimate reliability to reflect the way in which the scores for the writing samples are to be used in decision making. Thus, the procedure used to derive the examinees' scores should be taken into account in the estimation of reliability. For example, if examinees' scores are derived by summing or averaging the scores of multiple raters, the appropriate generalizability coefficient is estimated differently than it is if the score of a single rater is used.

Assessing Validity

Four different approaches have been used to estimate the validity of the ratings obtained from writing assessments. Breland (1983) offered a comprehensive review of validation studies of essay tests for college and secondary school students. Concurrent criterion-related validations have used such criteria as high school class rank, high school grade point average, English grades in college courses, cumulative college grade point average, and instructors' ratings of students' writing abilities. The range of the validity coefficients for sixteen studies conducted between 1954 and 1983 was .05–.43. Predictive validity coefficients, which used such criteria as grades in college English courses, semester grade point averages, and essay posttest scores, ranged from .21–.57. Breland's review further revealed that increments to validity were relatively modest when essay tests were used in conjuction with objective test scores and other predictors. However, Quellmalz (1984a) has suggested that the criteria used in such validation studies may be inadequate to represent the usefulness of direct writing assessments.

When writing assessments are used to assess instructional effectiveness or mastery of basic skills, it is appropriate to consider the content validity of the writing assessment tasks. Quellmalz (1984a) advocated using the same procedures for assessing the content validity of objectives and item specifications and the content validity of writing tasks and rating scales.

The concept of construct validity is appropriate to considerations of the issues of what trait or traits are measured by the writing tasks and scoring system. Several different types of studies seem relevant in the construct validation of writing tests. One approach is to examine whether holistic scores and analytic scores are a function of a common underlying trait. Chapman, Fyans, and Kerins (1984) have reported a construct validation of this type that used factor analysis. Breland (1983) noted that a central issue is whether direct and indirect measures of writing measure the same trait. The study conducted by Quellmalz, Capell, and Chou (1982) illustrates a third type of construct validation for writing tests. These researchers used confirmatory factor analysis to investigate whether different traits can be measured by different direct writing tasks. Finally, a thorough construct validation of a writing assessment should probably establish the extent to which essay scores are free from extraneous influences of variables that may be present in this situation. For example, handwriting has often been demonstrated to influence raters' judgments of essay quality (Chase, 1968, 1986). Context effect—that is, the effect of the quality of other essays read prior to the essay in question—have also been shown to affect essay scores (Daly and

Dickson-Markman, 1982; Hughes and Keeling, 1984). A thorough construct validation plan would include identification of extraneous variables and study of their impact on the scoring of writing samples.

Conclusion

Given the cost, the problems of establishing reliability and validity, and the time required to develop a sound writing assessment program, university and college educators and administrators may well ask, Is it worth it? In response, advocates of writing assessment point to the profound effects that such tests have had on secondary and college curricula and on classroom instructional practices. For example, Rentz (1984, p. 4) has described the impact of the inclusion of a writing test in the regents' testing program of the Georgia university system: "When the test was first administered in 1972, some colleges were abandoning freshman English composition as a requirement. Five years later, all colleges in the state required two composition courses, and about half these schools required three. Furthermore, the content of these courses consisted of writing, writing, writing. Instructional personnel were hired because they could teach writing. Faculty in other subject areas began to require writing. . . . It might be hard to solve some of the measurement problems, but direct assessment of writing by using a writing sample has credibility. The yield will be well worth the investment."

References

Breland, H. M. *The Direct Assessment of Writing Skill: A Measurement Review.* College Board Report no. 83-6, Educational Testing Service Research Report no. 83-32. Princeton, N.J.: Educational Testing Service, 1983.

Chapman, C. W., Fyans, L. J., Jr., and Kerins, C. T. "Writing Assessment in Illinois." *Educational Measurement Issues and Practice,* 1984, *3* (1), 24-26.

Chase, C. I. "The Impact of Some Obvious Variables on Essay Test Scores." *Journal of Educational Measurement,* 1968, *5* (4), 315-318.

Chase, C. I. "Essay Test Scoring: Interaction of Relevant Variables." *Journal of Educational Measurement,* 1986, *23* (1), 33-42.

Coffman, W. E. *Essay Examinations.* In R. L. Thorndike, *Educational Measurement.* (2nd ed.) Washington, D.C.: American Council on Education, 1971.

Crocker, L., and Algina, J. *Introduction to Classical and Modern Test Theory.* New York: Holt, Rinehart and Winston, 1986.

Daly, J. A., and Dickson-Markman, F. "Contrast Effects in Evaluating Essays." *Journal of Educational Measurement,* 1982, *19,* 309-316.

Diederich, P. B. *Measuring Growth in English.* Urbana, Ill.: National Council of Teachers of English, 1974.

Dovell, P., and Buhr, D. "Essay Topic Difficulty in Relation to Scoring Models." *Florida Journal of Educational Research,* 1986, *28,* 41-62.

Dubois, P. *A History of Psychological Testing.* Newton, Mass.: Allyn & Bacon, 1970.

Galton, F. "Classification of Men According to Their Natural Gifts." In W. Dennis (ed.), *Readings in the History of Psychology.* New York: Appleton-Century-Crofts, 1948.

Hoetker, J. "Essay Examination Topics and Students' Writing." *College Composition and Communication,* 1982, *37,* 377–392.

Hughes, D. C., and Keeling, B. "The Use of Model Essays to Reduce Context Effects in Essay Scoring." *Journal of Educational Measurement,* 1984, *21,* 277–282.

Llabre, M. M. "Application of Generalizability Theory to Assessment of Writing Ability." Unpublished doctoral dissertation, University of Florida, Gainesville, 1978.

Lloyd-Jones, R. "Primary Trait Scoring." In C. R. Cooper and L. Odell (eds.), *Evaluating Writing: Describing, Measuring, Judging.* Urbana, Ill.: National Council of Teachers of English, 1977.

Meredith, V. H., and Williams, P. L. "Issues in Direct Writing Assessment: Problem Identification and Control." *Educational Measurement Issues and Practice,* 1984, *3* (1), 11–15, 35.

Mullis, I. V. "Scoring Direct Writing Assessments: What Are the Alternatives?" *Educational Measurement Issues and Practice,* 1984, *3* (1), 16–18.

Quellmalz, E. S. "Designing Writing Assessments: Balancing Fairness, Utility, and Cost." *Educational Evaluation and Policy Analysis,* 1984a, *6* 63–72.

Quellmalz, E. S. "Toward Successful Large-Scale Writing Assessment: Where Are We Now? Where Do We Go from Here?" *Educational Measurement Issues and Practice,* 1984b, *3* (1), 29–32.

Quellmalz, E. S., Capell, F. J., and Chou, C. "Effects of Discourse and Response Mode on the Measurement of Writing Competence." *Journal of Educational Measurement,* 1982, *19,* 241–258.

Rentz, R. R. "Testing Writing by Writing." *Educational Measurement Issues and Practice,* 1984, *3* (1), 4.

Rosenbaum, P. R. *A Generalization of Direct Adjustment, with an Application to the Scaling of Essay Scores.* Technical Report no. 85-55. Princeton, N.J.: Educational Testing Service, 1985.

Sachse, P. P. "Writing Assessment in Texas: Practices and Problems." *Educational Measurement Issues and Practice,* 1984, *3* (1), 21–23.

Tate, G., Farmer, M., Gebhardt, R., King, M. L., Lied-Brilhart, B., Murray, B., Odell, L., and Tway, E. "Standards for Basic Skills Writing Programs." *Support for Learning and Teaching of English Newsletter (SLATE),* 1979, *4* (2), 1.

Linda Crocker is associate professor of education at the University of Florida, Gainesville.

*Because the proficiencies of entering students have declined
over the past twenty years, the need for placement testing
has increased greatly. This chapter discusses the factors to be
considered in developing assessment and placement programs:
which students should be tested, how testing should be carried
out, which tests should be used, and how tests should be
interpreted.*

A Primer
on Placement Testing

Edward A. Morante

The term *placement testing* is used in higher education to describe a process
of student assessment, the results of which are used to help to place entering
college students in appropriate beginning courses. While such a process has
existed at many colleges for years, the proficiencies of entering students
have declined over the past twenty years, and both the need for and the use
of placement tests has increased markedly. This chapter discusses which
students should be tested, when placement testing should be carried out,
and the variables that are important in selecting a placement test, and it
suggests a process for using tests in placement. It also discusses the compet-
ing claims of standardized and in-house tests, the issues of statewide testing,
and the rationale for placement testing.

Who Should Be Tested?

Who should be tested? The answer seems simple: All entering students who need or who would be helped by a course or by a level of a
course outside the regular college-level program. English and mathematics
are required at virtually every college, even in most certificate programs, but
we cannot assume that all students enter college at the same level of proficiency in these subjects. A placement test or a battery of tests is essential in

D. Bray, and M. J. Belcher (eds.). *Issues in Student Assessment.*
New Directions for Community Colleges, no. 59. San Francisco: Jossey-Bass, Fall 1987.

determining which courses or which levels of courses are most appropriate to individual students. Used in conjunction with other background information, test scores are essential in appropriate course placement. Individualized course placement is an essential step in retaining students.

Why Can Admissions Tests Not Be Used?

Admissions tests, like the Scholastic Aptitude Test (SAT) or the American College Test (ACT), are inappropriate for placement when used in isolation. They can be helpful in a comprehensive placement process if the results are considered in conjunction with scores on a placement test as well as other background information, but by themselves they provide insufficient and sometimes misleading information for placement.

The SAT and the ACT are designed to select among the brighter, more competent college applicants. While these tests differentiate among the better students, the task of a placement test is to differentiate among the less proficient students. The items on an admissions test and the items on a placement test are selected for these separate purposes. The time constraints are also different. As noted later in this chapter, placement tests should be unspeeded so that students can demonstrate how much they know, not how fast they can perform. The designers of admissions tests are interested in knowing both the level of a student's proficiency and the speed with which the student can demonstrate that proficiency, because the combination of knowledge and quickness is important in predicting success in college. Admissions tests are thus more closely aligned with aptitude tests, which assess how capable a prospective student is of learning. Placement tests should be used to measure proficiency, not aptitude or capability, and they should not be used to predict future success.

The SAT and the ACT are inappropriate as sole placement devices also because they do not accurately measure proficiency in basic skills. In New Jersey, for example, the Basic Skills Council compared SAT results with the results of the New Jersey College Basic Skills Placement Test (NJCBSPT). The council found that many students with above-average SAT scores were still not proficient enough in basic skills to be ready for college-level courses. The conclusion of this analysis, which was first carried out in 1978 and then repeated in 1986, was that a placement test was needed for accurate placement even for students who performed above the national average on the SAT.

Why Can High School Grades Not Be Used?

High school grades can and should be used in making placement decisions, but only in conjunction with a placement test. High school grades, the type and number of courses taken in high school, grade point average, and rank in class are all helpful variables in making placement decisions. However, there are two reasons why none of these indicators, used alone or in combination, is sufficient. First, many students (the so-called nontraditional students) have been away from high school for a number of years. Their high school performance may not accurately measure their current proficiencies. This issue appears to be especially important for mathematics, which many students seem to forget if they do not use it regularly.

Second, high school transcripts can be difficult to interpret, and they are sometimes even contradictory. Different schools, programs, teachers, and courses provide little continuity, which is necessary for understanding and measuring the proficiencies of students. While the fact that one student lacks certain courses may indicate that the student's proficiency in that area is apt to be low, the fact that another student has successfully completed what appear to be appropriate high school courses in the area is no guarantee of the student's proficiency. This is true even for recent high school graduates of a college preparatory curriculum. For example, the New Jersey Basic Skills Council (1986) found that only 2.5 percent of the recent high school graduates who had successfully completed a college preparatory mathematics curriculum were proficient in elementary algebra and that fully 50 percent of the students could not successfully answer even half of the algebra problems on the test where the most difficult question was of the form $ax = c - bx$, solve for x. Indeed, 36 percent of the same students could not successfully answer nineteen of the thirty questions on an arithmetic test that measures proficiency in fractions, decimals, and percents. It is beyond the scope of this chapter to explain these results. Let it suffice to say that it is risky to rely on high school performance as a measure of proficiency in the making of placement decisions. Thus, the use of a test specifically designed for placement is essential.

In-House and Standardized Tests

The development of basic skills placement tests by local faculty is widespread. The resulting tests are generally referred to as *in-house tests.* While the writing of an essay topic or of mathematics problems appears to be relatively easy, most faculty seem to agree that the development of a reading test or a multiple-choice writing test lies beyond the capabilities of most local groups.

This consensus masks a deeper problem. While the writing of items or questions appears to be relatively simple for some, especially for those who have taught for many years, the writing of good, unambiguous items that discriminate well among students of different groups, that are unbiased, and that relate well to the total test score is much more complex than it appears to be on the surface. In addition, the combination of items to form a comprehensive test that is both reliable and valid is very difficult to accomplish without a process of pretesting, statistical analysis, and objective, professional review. In addition, the development of alternate forms, which is important for retesting and posttesting, requires a level of sophisticated psychometrics that most faculty do not have or do not use in developing an in-house test.

The biggest complaint that faculty make against standardized tests seems to be that such tests do not measure what they want students to know or that the tests do not measure what faculty teach. However, the same complaint could be made against standardized tests, depending both on which test was selected and on what was taught in the curriculum. In-house tests can be written to reflect a selected curriculum, but they may not provide accurate measurement. Faculty and administrators need to review the advantages and disadvantages of these two types of tests for the purpose of placement.

Selecting a Placement Test

The selection of an appropriate placement test is one of the most important factors in a comprehensive developmental education program. The placement test and the cut scores that are used cannot be differentiated from the standards of quality set by the college. Nine factors should be considered in any decision about a particular placement test, including an in-house test: the test's content, referencing, discrimination, speededness, reliability, validity, and cost; its control for guessing; and the availability of alternate forms.

Content is the most critical variable in decisions about the quality of placement tests. The test or test battery should include reading, writing, and mathematics. It can address other areas as well, depending on the needs of individual programs or institutions. The reading component should be realistic and holistic. The topics or passages should cover a range of subject matter. Comprehension, understanding, and inferential reasoning are essential. The vocabulary should be in context. Standards should be set no lower than the equivalent of eleventh grade.

The writing component should have both an essay and a multiple-choice section. The essay should be expository and require the student to demonstrate reasoning and organizational skills (for example, take a position and defend it with examples) as well as mastery of the mechanics of English (grammar, syntax, punctuation, spelling, and capitalization). The multiple-choice section should assess the student's understanding of English in context, not merely the student's ability to identify the mechanics of English in isolation. Standards should be set no lower than the equivalent of eleventh grade.

Arithmetic (computation) and elementary algebra are essential in the mathematics component. Higher levels may be appropriate. The arithmetic questions should involve both problem solving and word problems and make use of fractions, decimals, and percentages. Estimation problems are essential for measuring the understanding of concepts. The algebra items should consist both of problems and of word problems and at the minimum include linear equations involving numeral, fractional, and literal components. Assessment of vocabulary is not important.

A good placement test is criterion referenced. That is, levels of difficulty and proficiency should be established by faculty judgments of what students should know, not by norm-referenced procedures based on the skills that students bring at entry.

A good placement test has discriminatory power. That is, it can differentiate accurately among students along a continuum of proficiency. Discrimination is essential in decisions about the need for remedial or developmental education and within levels of basic skills courses. A placement test should discriminate best among students with low proficiencies.

A good placement test is a power test. Speed should not be an important factor. Time limits are appropriate only for administrative purposes. The rule of thumb is that 100 percent of the students should complete at least 75 percent of the items, and 90 percent of the students should attempt all the items.

The reliability of a test can be defined as the likelihood that a student will achieve the same score if the student takes the test again. (The assumption is that the student receives no treatment between administrations.) Test-retest and split-half reliability are the methods most often used. Reliability coefficient should be at least .90. (Kuder-Richardson -20 coefficients are inflated by the length of the test and speededness.)

The validity of a test can be defined as the likelihood that the test in fact measures what it is supposed to measure. The validity of a test includes its face validity (the degree to which the test looks as if it measures what it is supposed to measure), concurrent validity (the test's relationship to other, similar tests), and predictive validity (the degree to which the test predicts or correlates with some criterion, such as course grades). The predictive validity of placement tests is difficult to judge, because correlations between placement test scores and grades in a remedial or development course that functions well should approach zero.

Guessing, an error factor in multiple-choice tests and in most other kinds of tests, imperils the accuracy of placement decisions. Because guessing can only inflate scores, some tests compensate for it by including a factor that systematically lowers scores. The effects of random guessing can be limited by increasing the number of choices (four or five are considerably better than two) and by directing students accordingly.

Every placement test should have an equivalent alternate form that can be used both for retesting when necessary and for posttesting.

Cost is the last variable that needs to be considered. The cost of a test includes the cost of materials, administration, and scoring. Placement tests should be able to be scored both by machine and by hand.

Using Tests in Placement Decisions

The term *cut scores* refers to a test score that is used to differentiate student performance for the purpose of making placement decisions. Since multiple levels of developmental education should be employed at most colleges, multiple levels of cut scores should also be determined. In fact, since no one score is sufficient for making decisions, it would be more accurate to speak instead of cut ranges.

The traditional method of establishing cut scores is to correlate test scores with grades. This method necessitates placing virtually all students in college-level courses at least initially in order to collect the data needed for the statistical analysis. Of course, this is probably not appropriate, since many of the students who need developmental courses would (or should) perform poorly if placed directly in college-level courses. The price of high failure rates to establish a statistically based system of cut scores in unacceptable to most people.

The following steps offer a practical method of setting placement cutoff ranges that are methodologically sound and that do not increase the probability of student failure: First, select a task force or committee of faculty and appropriate administrators. Make judgments about the test scores on the placement test that are needed for a determination of proficiency. (Past cut scores or national norms can be used at first until more information is collected.) Second, assume three levels of proficiency for each skills area: the level of those who clearly do not need remediation, the level of those who clearly need remediation, and the level of those in the large "grey" area between these two extremes. It is in this middle area that other factors beyond the placement test scores become increasingly important. Third, in systems where levels of remediation exist, establish similar cut score ranges for each level offered. Fourth, use this system of cut score ranges to place students in developmental courses. Fifth, after two to four weeks, collect ratings from course instructors about the success of the placement decisions. Ensure that faculty members have rated students on proficiency and not on other areas, such as class attendance, participation, or attitude. Instructors should make these ratings without knowing the students' placement test scores. Sixth, use the information provided by the faculty ratings to adjust the cut scores. Change student placements where appropriate and feasible, but be conservative.

The importance of establishing grey areas cannot be overstated. Tests are not perfect, and single scores on one test are considerably less than perfect. Accurate and reliable placement decisions can be made only if multiple factors are used. At the minimum, seven factors should be considered: placement test scores, other available test information, high school data, other background data, age, student opinion, and results of additional testing.

Both placement test scores and the consistency of placement test scores should be considered. Scores that fall well above or well below the cut range have a relatively high probability of being accurate and should weigh more heavily than scores that fall in the grey middle area. Similarly, consistent scores (for example, a low essay score combined with a low multiple-choice writing score) are probably more accurate than conflicting scores.

The other available test information that should figure in placement decisions can include SAT or ACT scores and scores from any other tests, including in-class tests and diagnostic tests, that have been administered. Decision makers should look for consistent patterns in the student's test scores.

Information about the school attended, number and kinds of courses taken, and high school rank can be helpful. However, there is little consistency in the data obtained from different schools and even from different courses within the same school.

The other background data that should be considered include such factors as years since high school, jobs and work activities, financial situation, and extracurricular activities. As a general rule, the more responsibilities and difficulties a student faces in his or her personal life, the greater the likelihood that the student will require developmental education, a relatively light course load, or both.

Age is a relevant factor in placement decisions in the following way: Older students tend to be more fearful, more cautious, and more motivated. Thus, everything else being equal, older students probably have a better chance of success in college courses than younger students.

Student opinion becomes a relevant factor in placement decisions only when other factors are confusing, contradictory, or inconclusive. Many students, especially recent high school graduates, tend to overestimate their abilities.

Additional testing can help to clarify conflicting information from other sources. Retest results should only be used in the context supplied by the other data. Diagnostic testing should be used only to identify specific skills areas, not to reverse placement decisions.

Pros and Cons of Statewide Placement Testing

A growing number of states either have initiated (for example, New Jersey, Tennessee, Florida) or are now considering (for example, Texas, Georgia, California) mandatory basic skills placement testing for all students entering public college systems. What are the advantages and and disadvantages of a statewide effort in this area?

The Southern Regional Education Board (SREB, 1986) surveyed the placement tests and cut scores used by colleges in its fifteen-state region. It found that more than a hundred different tests were used and that the cut scores ranged from a low of the first percentile to a high of the ninety-fourth percentile. How can standards be comparable in the face of such divergence?

It could be argued that such differences exemplify the variety of the missions of the American higher education system. But, does this rationale for diversity hold when we attempt to define the basic skills of the students who enter college? Should there be a floor, a minimum standard in basic skills proficiency that every college should demand for its college-level courses? While the answer to this question does not necessarily lead to a statewide measure, a statewide test would make it necessary to reach some agreement both about what should be measured and at what level. The establishment of a state standard or at least of a floor leads to an understanding of the meaning of proficiency, to the setting of a minimum standard. Of course, the fact that institutions have different missions can and should allow for the establishment of cut scores higher than the minimum.

There is an additional concern about basing standards only on a local or individual institution that can be described as the norm-referenced phenomenon, namely the tendency to set standards according to the proficiencies of the students who come to the institution. This tendency can jeopardize both quality and standards when a college sets its cut scores at a predetermined level based on some a priori percentage of the number of students who should or can be accommodated in developmental or remedial courses (for example, one quarter or one third). The use of a statewide standard helps faculty to select criteria according to what proficiency in basic skills is judged to be, regardless of the college in which a student enrolls or of the proficiencies of entering students at that school. This allows the program to be adjusted according to the needs of the students, not of the standards.

Feedback to the high schools is the third important reason for establishing a statewide testing program. Only if there is a standardized statewide examination for all entering freshmen can meaningful information on the proficiencies of graduating students be sent to the high schools of the state. It is impossible to interpret the results of differing tests that use differing levels of proficiency and content in any meaningful way. It is unlikely that anything can be more powerful in this regard than the results of a statewide test of basic skills proficiency.

Decreases in costs, increases in communication (within colleges, across different colleges and sections of higher education, and between K–12 and postsecondary education), and data for reform are all important variables that support the need for statewide testing. While statewide basic skills testing is not necessary for effective course placement, it provides a powerful mechanism for establishing educational standards as well as a strong catalyst for reform.

Conclusion

Placement testing is an essential ingredient of a successful college program. The diversity of background and proficiency that students bring to our colleges demands individual attention and course selection. To dump everyone in the same level of course is significantly to increase the probability either of lowering standards or of failing many students. The test that is selected and the cut scores that are used play important roles in access, retention, and quality. Colleges need to place as much emphasis on the careful selection of a placement test as they do on curriculum development and student recruitment. Any college that does not recognize the interaction will pay a high price, and so will its students.

References

New Jersey State Department of Higher Education. *Results of the New Jersey College Basic Skills Placement Testing, Fall 1985.* Trenton: New Jersey Basic Skills Council, New Jersey State Department of Higher Education, 1986. 71 pp. (ED 269 059)
Southern Regional Education Board. *College-Level Study. What Is It? Variations in College Placement Tests and Standards in the SREB States.* Issues in Higher Education, no. 2. Atlanta, Ga.: Southern Regional Education Board, 1986.

Edward A. Morante is director of the College Outcomes Evaluation Program in the New Jersey Department of Higher Education.

Accommodating testing situations to disabled students presents
special challenges for the administration and interpretation
of test results. This chapter provides some background
information on the testing of disabled students and presents
results from a recent survey of efforts in California to deal
with this issue.

Accommodating Testing
to Disabled Students

Emmett Casey

The community colleges face a critical juncture during the 1980s. The preceding two decades were periods of tremendous growth and expansion for postsecondary education. However, higher education is now experiencing enrollment declines, budget restrictions, and competition for students. In an effort to maintain open access, community colleges accept all the students they can. Recent studies indicate that persons with disabilities of college age are attending postsecondary institutions in increasing numbers (Black, 1982). While continuing to make college attractive and accessible, community colleges also want to provide the opportunity for success. To accomplish these goals of access and success, more assessment of potential students, including students with disabilities, is taking place.

Community colleges are using considerably more testing for admissions, placement, and related academic activities than they did in the past (Woods, 1985). The administration of such tests has an impact on all students, but it may have a significant impact on students with disabilities. Because much of the testing is new, few data are available on what tests are being given and on whether and how testing is being accommodated to the needs of students with disabilities.

Section 504 of the 1973 Rehabilitation Act requires that testing be adapted for disabled students so that it measures what it is designed to

D. Bray, and M. J. Belcher (eds.). *Issues in Student Assessment.*
New Directions for Community Colleges, no. 59. San Francisco: Jossey-Bass, Fall 1987.

measure while allowing for the student's disability. The prevailing philosophy among the people who work with disabled students and among disabled students themselves is that academic standards must be maintained while appropriate accommodations in test administration are made. The attitudes among faculty, administrators, and students as well as the general public can range from the position that disabled students should have to take tests under the same conditions as other students to demonstrate that they belong in school to the position that disabled students should not have to take tests at all. It seems likely that there is a valid middle ground somewhere between these extremes.

The literature that followed passage of Section 504 of the 1973 Rehabilitation Act focused on ensuring the rights of disabled students and reinforced the need for testing accommodation (Federal Register, 1980). Yet, the literature has little to say about how postsecondary education can accommodate disabled students in the area of testing. An Educational Resources Information Center (ERIC) search using the descriptors *disabilities, postsecondary education,* and *admissions* turned up five articles. The descriptors *disabilities, postsecondary education,* and *student recruitment* yielded sixteen articles, and the descriptors *disabilities, postsecondary education,* and *college entrance examinations* yielded only one.

The Office of Civil Rights published a guide for activities that would assist in complying with Section 504. The section relating to admission tests states: "Some of the questions and issues raised by testing have not been resolved in a manner that will allow useful guidelines at this time" (Redden, Levering, and DiQuinzio, 1978, p. 21). In 1981, the Association of Handicapped Student Service Programs in Postsecondary Education (AHSSPPE) sponsored a conference on the accessible institution of higher education. Questions regarding the validation of alternative tests, concerns about the identification and accommodation of learning disabilities, and issues of standardized tests were addressed. It was noted that there are no "fully developed test modifications suitable for all handicapped individuals, nor is there information about the comparability of available tests for the handicapped" (Sherman, 1981, p. 68).

The lack of information and knowledge extends from the professionals in the field to disabled persons as well. Ragosta (1981) examined how disabled students perceived the SAT with its modifications. Her findings revealed that few disabled students were even aware of the possibility of special administrations of standardized tests.

Test Validity and Accommodation

Testing the handicapped leads to a quandary from which there are few avenues of escape. Most of the tests used for admission to college have norms and standardized procedures. When special accommodations based on disability alter the standardized procedure, the validity of the test may be called into question. However, if the standardized procedure is followed, the learning potential or achievement of the disabled person may be underestimated.

In some instances, tests may be waived for disabled students because of this problem. For example, a law passed in Massachusetts in 1983 freed high school students with dyslexia and other language learning disabilities from having to take aptitude tests in order to gain admission to state colleges and universities. In instances where accommodations are made for the disabled students, the results are "red flagged" to indicate that procedures other than the standardized ones were used, for example, that the time allowed for completing the test was extended. This practice could tend to draw attention to the disabled student, and it may be discriminatory. It also makes the results difficult to interpret.

The solution is not much clearer if testing is to be continued. One possible way of resolving the quandary is to use the same tests but to adapt the procedures in a standardized fashion. Separate norms for the disabled would then be used to interpret test scores. The alternative is totally separate tests based on disability.

The type of disability would dictate the possible accommodation. Students who are legally blind or who have serious vision problems may require taped tests, large-print tests, tests in braille, or persons to read the tests and record the students' responses. These students may require a special setting or equipment so that the testing mode would not distract other students taking tests. However, problems arise if part of the exam requires students to interpret printed charts and graphs, which are difficult to describe verbally. Mathematics may also be difficult to accommodate in this mode.

Deaf students may require test instructions to be given in sign language but be expected to read the exam and answer the questions. In such a situation, a deaf student with an English language deficiency might score lower than he or she would if the test had been administered completely in sign language. Deaf students may do much better in the mathematics component if the problems are not word problems but computations and calculations.

Two large national testing services, Educational Testing Service (ETS) and the American College Testing Program (ACT), are interested in the issue of testing disabled students. Studies of admissions testing and disabled individuals have been undertaken by the College Board, the Graduate Record Examinations Board, and ETS, and two reports have resulted (Bennett and Ragosta, 1985; Bennett, Ragosta, and Stricker, 1985). The authors found considerable disagreement in the field of special education about the definitions of particular disabilities, especially about learning disabilities. This disagreement causes serious problems for researchers.

In addition, few disabled are administered standardized admissions tests, such as the Scholastic Aptitude Test (SAT). In the 1982-83 school year, 4.2 million students—approximately 10 percent of the entire public school population—were classified as handicapped by the nation's elementary and secondary schools. Yet, only approximately 6,000 of the 1.5 million students who took the SAT requested special administration. The overwhelming majority (4,300) of those who requested special administration were learning disabled. Why were the handicapped so underrepresented? Is it a problem with definition, or is it merely lack of knowledge that special administrations are available? Perhaps few handicapped are considering further education, or perhaps they are admitted to colleges that waive test requirements. Further research is needed.

However, despite the definitional problems and the small numbers, the admissions testing surveyed by Bennett and Ragosta (1985) and Bennett, Ragosta, and Stricker (1985) indicates that students with physical or visual disabilities performed similar to, but at a level slightly lower than, nondisabled peers. Learning-disabled students performed at levels significantly below those of nondisabled peers. Students with hearing disabilities performed least well as a group, and they performed better on mathematical measures than they did on verbal ones. Last, students who performed poorly on admissions tests did poorly in college, and students who performed well on admissions tests did well in college, whether they were disabled or not.

California Community Colleges Survey of Testing Accommodation for Disabled Students

California has one of the largest configurations of community colleges in the world, with approximately 1.5 million students. With this number, there are approximately 50,000 disabled students or almost 3.5 percent of the student population. California is also one of the leaders, if not the leader, in providing special funding for programs for disabled students at the postsecondary level. For these reasons, it seemed appropriate to survey what the community colleges in California were doing with respect to testing and accommodation for students with disabilities.

Purpose and Scope of Survey. A study was conducted in order to answer the following questions: Are testing accommodations being made for disabled students? What accommodations are currently being made and for whom? What other accommodations might be made and for whom? Are disabled students waived from taking tests, and if so, which students? Last, what types of tests are being used for placement?

Procedure. Figure 1 shows the survey form that was developed to elicit answers to the questions just stated (Figure 1 also tabulates the survey results.) It was based on a form developed by the New York University

Figure 1. Survey Form for the California Community Colleges Survey of Testing Accommodation for Disabled Students

Please answer the following questions regarding testing and disabled students on your campus.

1. Does your college currently have testing for class placement?

        97% Yes   3% No

2. If yes, does your college have special accommodations for disabled students?

        98% Yes   1% No

3. If your college does not currently make accommodations for testing disabled students, what accommodations do you think they might make in the future for testing?

4. Are accommodations made for classroom exams, such as quizzes, lab exams, oral presentations?

        98% Yes _____ No

5. If yes, please indicate what types of accommodations are made. Mark all that apply.
   - 94% Time limit extended
   - 94% Exam administered in a special location
   - 83% Answers recorded in any manner, e.g. typewriter, computer, or tape recorder
   - 46% Use of calculator
   - 94% Questions read or interpreted (sign language)
   - 75% Exam provided in braille, large print, or on tape
   - 10% Questions omitted, credit prorated
   - 22% Other _____

                          (please specify)

6. Are disabled students waived from taking tests?

        14% Yes   85% No

7. If yes, please mark the types of disabled students for whom waivers are granted. Mark all that apply.
   - 4% Deaf
   - 3% Blind
   - 3% Physically disabled
   - 4% Specific learning disabled
   - 3% Developmentally disabled
   - 3% Other _____

                          (please specify)

8. What types of placement testing do you currently use?
   - _____ New Jersey Test of Basic Skills (NJTBS)
   - 10% ASSET
   - 10% Other _____

                          (please specify)

9. In your opinion, on a scale of 1 to 5, how important is placement testing? Please mark below.

Very Important				Not Important
5	4	3	2	1
20	9	5	1	1

Comments:

Office for Education of Children with Handicapping Conditions in March 1982. The form was field-tested by colleagues in the community colleges, and their input was used to clarify and refine it further. The form was then sent by the Office of Specially Funded Programs of the Community Colleges State Chancellor to all 106 community colleges in the state. The survey was addressed to deans of students, since it was felt that most college testing programs would fall under their jurisdiction. Recipients were instructed to return the completed form to San Diego for processing.

One hundred and one of the 106 colleges (95 percent) completed the survey. One college returned two copies of the form, one completed by the dean and one by the head of the disabled students program. Their responses were different, and both copies of the form were included in the analysis.

Results. Community colleges in California give placement tests to their students and provide special accommodations for disabled students. Almost all the colleges (97 percent) reported that they were testing for class placement, and of these colleges, 98 percent said they had special accommodations for disabled students.

Table 1 shows how the accommodations made in placement testing vary by disability. For visual impairment, most respondents extend time limits (85 percent) or administer the exam in a special location (89 percent). Surprisingly, only about two thirds stated that they accommodated visual impairments by reading questions or by providing a copy of the exam in braille or large print or a copy recorded on tape. Fewer accommodations are made for those who are physically impaired with motor difficulties, although a large percentage receive extended time and special locations. Students with specific learning disabilities and hearing impairments are often accommodated by extending time limits and providing a special location, but the incidence of accommodation for these students is lower than it is for both visual and physical impairment.

When the responses of those who said they were willing to make accommodations in the future are added to the category of accommodations currently being made, we can see a trend toward unanimous approval for having colleges accommodate students with disabilities at least in some fashion. Administrators are most likely to provide extra time and appear least likely to allow the use of a calculator, either currently or in the future. Greater leeway in allowing this device might have been expected, especially for the learning-disabled students.

The placement tests used at the colleges where these accommodations are being made are typically the College Board Comparative Guidance and Placement Program (CGP) and the American College Testing Program's ASSET for reading and writing. About 50 percent of the respondents used one of these measures in reading, and 47 percent did so for writing. In math, 25 percent reported using one of these two tests, while another 21 percent used a locally developed test.

Table 1. Alternative Testing Techniques Used for Disabled Students

Student Disability/ Learner Characteristics	Time Limit Extended		Exam Administered in a Special Location		Answers Recorded on Tape Recorder, Dictaphone, Typewriter		Use of a Calculator Allowed		Questions Read or Interpreted by Sign Language		Exam Copy Provided in Braille or Large Print or on Tape	
	Currently Done	Possible in Future	Currently Done	Possible in Future	Currently Done	Possible in Future	Currently Done	Possible in Future	Currently Done	Possible in Future	Currently Done	Possible in Future
Visual impairment	85%	7%	89%	4%	45%	19%	29%	11%	66%	6%	64%	22%
Physical impairment with motor difficulties	82%	9%	80%	6%	44%	18%	24%	8%	25%	4%	12%	7%
Health impairment	60%	8%	60%	10%	26%	13%	18%	10%	18%	5%	12%	7%
Specific learning disabilities	73%	8%	74%	6%	38%	20%	28%	12%	53%	5%	28%	13%
Hearing impaired with language difficulties	69%	8%	65%	9%	13%	11%	14%	8%	64%	13%	9%	5%
Speech impairment	35%	7%	35%	10%	14%	12%	9%	7%	11%	7%	7%	6%

To the questions of how important placement testing was, approximately one third of the respondents thought that it was of some importance. A very small percent (2 percent) considered it to be of no importance. The majority of the respondents did not answer the question.

Various accommodations are also being used in the classroom to test disabled students. In response to the question, Are accommodations made for classroom exams, for example, quizzes, lab exams, oral presentations? 98 percent said yes. To the question, Are disabled students waived from taking tests? 85 percent said no. It seems to make sense that waivers are not necessary if accommodation is being made. Only a very small percentage of the respondents indicated that waivers were granted for any type of disability.

In the classroom, the most frequent accommodation (94 percent) was to extend time limits and administer the exam in a special location. Reading questions to students or interpreting them in sign language occurred more often in the classroom than it did in the standardized testing situation. In rank order based on the percentage of responses, the other accommodations that were reported were answers recorded in any manner (83 percent), exam provided in braille or large print or on tape (75 percent), use of calculator allowed (46 percent), other (22 percent), questions omitted, credit prorated (10 percent).

What are the implications of the willingness of colleges to accommodate students with disabilities? It appears that the twin goals of access and success alluded to earlier for community colleges in California are being realized through the effort to accommodate students with disabilities.

Summary and Recommendations

Testing the growing population of disabled students is a difficult issue. Solutions that are suitable in all cases have yet to be found. In the meantime, disabled students are often tested under a variety of accommodations. However, the results lack precise meaning whenever comparisons are made and predictions are needed. Nevertheless, the following recommendations can be made for the testing and accommodation to be provided for students with disabilities in the future: First, indicators other than actual testing—for example, letters from previous teachers indicating skill levels and types of accommodation needed for successful completion of courses—should be accepted for placement decisions. Second, "standardized" methods for the administration of tests should be developed for each disability category. This recommendation might mean administering tests to the blind via tape recording in a special location or substituting an art history class for a visual arts type of class if such a class is required for graduation or a diploma. The test would not include the use of graphs or charts. Third, rather than basing placement decisions exclusively on test scores, colleges should allow disabled students to try a class at what is agreed to be the most likely level of placement. If that level is subsequently shown to be inappropriate, the necessary adjustments can still be made. Fourth, practice tests should be provided to give students with disabilities an opportunity to improve their performance. Fifth, collaboration between K-12 schools and colleges or continuing education facilities should become closer to help disabled students make the transition. Sixth, the use of advisory groups of disabled persons to review modifications of procedures, accommodations, or newly developed tests should increase. Seventh, disabled students should become more involved in planning by local state departments of rehabilitation. This recommendation may also help with the problem of identifying learning-disabled students and determining eligibility for learning disabilities services. Last, programs of public awareness should be increased so that disabled students as well as the general public know what accommodations are available.

References

Bennett, R. E., and Ragosta, M. *A Research Context for Studying Admissions Tests and Handicapped Populations.* Studies of Admissions Testing and Handicapped People, Report no. 1. New York: College Entrance Examination Board; Princeton, N.J.: Educational Testing Service and Graduate Record Examinations Board, 1985. 90 pp. (ED 251 485)

Bennett, R. E., Ragosta, M., and Stricker, L. J. *The Test Performance of Handicapped People.* Studies of Admissions Testing and Handicapped People, Report no. 2. New York: College Entrance Examination Board; Princeton, N.J.: Educational Testing Service; Knoxville: Department of Distributive Education, University of Tennessee, 1985. 54 pp. (ED 251 487)

Black L. K. "Handicapped Needs Assessment." *Community College/Junior College Quarterly of Research and Practice,* 1982, *6* (4), 355-369.

Ragosta, M. "Handicapped Students and Standardized Tests." In S. H. Simon (ed.), *The Accessible Institution of Higher Education: Opportunity, Challenge, and Response.* Ames, Iowa: Association of Handicapped Student Service Programs in Postsecondary Education, 1981. 245 pp. (ED 216 487)

Redden, M. R., Levering, C., and DiQuinzio, D. *Recruitment, Admissions, and Handicapped Students.* Washington, D.C.: U.S. Department of Health, Education, and Welfare, 1978.

Sherman, S. W. "Issues in the Testing of Handicapped People." In S. H. Simon (ed.), *The Accessible Institution of Higher Education: Opportunity, Challenge, and Response.* Ames, Iowa: Association on Handicapped Student Service Programs in Postsecondary Education, 1981. 245 pp. (ED 216 487)

United States National Archives and Record Service. *Federal Register.* Washington, D.C.: Office of the Federal Register, National Archives and Record Service, 1980.

Woods, J. E. *Status of Testing Practices at Two-Year Postsecondary Institutions.* Iowa City, Iowa: American College Testing Program; Washington, D.C.: American Association of Community and Junior Colleges, 1985, 73 pp. (ED 264 907)

The state of Florida uses several forms of assessment to improve the quality of public higher education.

The Impact of Assessment on Minority Access

Roy E. McTarnaghan

Assessment in Florida's postsecondary institutions focuses on taking stock of student achievement at periodic intervals, improving guidance and placement for appropriate course experiences, improving feedback to secondary schools on college-level performance so that strengths and weaknesses can be noted, increasing college readiness for applicants from secondary schools, improving the likelihood of retention and success in college, and measuring college-level skills at the end of the second college year. A variety of intervention strategies have been developed, some by way of legislative initiative; others were identified in the master plans of the three public higher education boards: the Postsecondary Education Planning Commission, the Board of Regents, and the State Board for Community Colleges. All groups are committed to quality control and quality improvement.

Now, nearly ten years after this series of actions started, evidence is beginning to mount that setting reasonable goals, communicating them effectively, and giving faculty the responsibility for developing standards and assessment techniques have made a positive contribution to quality control in higher education. At the same time, a high level of sensitivity to the potential for negative impact on minority access has challenged the state to improve its record in this regard.

A formal series of assessment measures is in place in Florida, both

D. Bray, and M. J. Belcher (eds.). *Issues in Student Assessment.*
New Directions for Community Colleges, no. 59. San Francisco: Jossey-Bass, Fall 1987.

in the public schools and at the college and university level. These measures range from requiring elementary and secondary school basic skills tests and minimum achievement levels in reading, writing, mathematics, and application of skills to daily life to tightening graduation requirements, using placement exams, making grade information from college available to secondary schools, and measuring achievement at the end of the lower-division core courses in college. These changes did not all occur together, nor were they even linked in the original plan. Rather, they evolved out of a concern to improve education, to regain the public trust, and to recover what had been lost: the idea that a diploma or degree represented achievement and mastery, not just time spent in classrooms. The discovery that minority students were less likely to be in a college preparatory curriculum, more likely to be counseled into vocational programs, and more likely to be ill-prepared and thus to fail in college degree programs was another part of this evolution. The open door looked to many minority students like a swinging door, quick in and quick out. Florida's assessment programs have been designed to be useful, helpful, and supportive of the educational process. The mandated programs have been designed to specify objectives, see that students know what is expected, use assessment to evaluate readiness, provide periodic feedback, and certify achievement at specified levels. Questions will always be raised about the level of achievement or performance that is selected, but procedures are in place to monitor and to recommend changes as needed.

In order to support improvement in educational programs and student achievement and to assure that assessment is used constructively to increase minority access, states need to build a data base that enables them to observe how assessment is being used, how changes are made, and what data are available for applications, admissions, enrollment, attrition, retention, and degrees earned. A feedback loop is necessary to evaluate present plans and to adjust them in order to build on areas of success and eliminate problem areas. It must be clear that the improvement of minority access is an integral part of any assessment program. The Florida legislature has funded a number of assessment programs, and it and the state board of education, together with the State Board for Community Colleges and the Board of Regents, require regular reporting.

Historical Development

Florida's public system of higher education has been characterized since 1965 by a formal transfer arrangement between two-year community colleges and four-year universities. The community colleges have been primarily open access, while access to the universities has been limited both by admission standards and by a pre-established enrollment plan. In this environment, of every hundred students enrolled over the last ten years as entering freshmen in public higher education, seventy-eight have entered a community college, and twenty-two have entered a university.

The formal articulation agreement between the two sectors provides for transfer to the junior year in the university system for any student who completes the associate of arts degree at one of Florida's twenty-eight community colleges. The core of general education is accepted in this transfer as a package, and the individual courses in the degree program are not an issue. In the context described here, assessment in the community colleges had for many years focused on guidance and placement for the entering student, while in the university it was generally thought of as part of the admissions process.

Core academic high school units that were part of graduation requirements when the 1965 articulation agreement was signed were eroded when the state minimum standards were phased out and replaced by local district guidelines. During the 1970s, the number of college preparatory courses taken by graduating high school seniors dropped significantly, and the public expressed concern over the perceived quality of the high school diploma. Without imposing course requirements, the legislature began in 1976 to impose assessment tests to measure basic skills among those qualifying for graduation. A state-developed test, the Florida Twelfth-Grade Test, had been used for many years in combination with high school performance to predict the student's college performance for entry into the state university system. Allegations of discriminatory use of this instrument and charges that the test was racially biased led the Florida legislature to stop funding the program.

Admissions to State Universities

Against this background, validation studies were conducted in the state university system using secondary school performance and nationally normed admissions test. Analysis of entering freshman applicants between 1978 and 1980 showed that fewer than one quarter had completed what had been considered a college preparatory program some fifteen years earlier. Further, black students appeared to be placed in non–college preparatory courses in such large numbers that no more than 10 percent were in the traditional sequence geared for college.

Conventional studies of efforts to predict college success in the entering year had shown that the core academic courses were generally a better predictor than an admissions test. Florida studies in the period around 1980 continued to show that the tendency prevailed for white students and that it was less predictive for Hispanic and black students. This analysis suggested that the higher correlation between the admissions test and achieved grade point average in college could be due in part to the fact that large numbers of minority students enrolled in non–college preparatory courses. A review of several thousand high school transcripts in 1980 for admission to the state university system confirmed that minority students had been exposed on the average to one to two units less in mathematics and science than majority students had. While the differences in English and in the social sciences were not great, placement appeared to be made between and among sections to focus on college-bound and non-college-bound students; minorities were more numerous among the non-college-bound groups.

The result was that the Board of Regents of the state university system endorsed increased admissions standards in 1981. The increased standards called for higher score levels on the two nationally normed admissions tests as well as increases in the number and type of college preparatory courses; the course requirements were to rise in three phases—1981, 1984, and 1986. The regents also encouraged close counseling and advisement ties between higher education and public schools so as to encourage minorities to enroll in courses and programs that would help them to succeed in college. Florida had secured an agreement with the United States Office for Civil Rights in 1978 on a plan aimed at increasing minority participation in postsecondary education, and the two-year and four-year colleges were linked in the effort. What effect would raising standards have on the challenge to increase the numbers? An important provision of the admissions policy for the university system was to provide for exceptions as needed in order to meet minority enrollment goals. As the policy was carried out, special support services were developed at the institutional level to provide reinforcement for less well-prepared students.

College-Level Academic Skills Test

In the early 1980s, the Florida legislature mandated the development of an assessment program called the College-Level Academic Skills Test (CLAST). This program, which involved community college and university faculty in the computation and communication areas, specified college sophomore–level competencies in computation, reading, writing, and essay. By 1984, statewide standards were in place as a factor in qualifying for the associate in arts degree or for moving to the upper division in a state university. The same standards must be achieved for the bachelor's degree. The cutoff scores for these standards were increased in 1984, and 1986, and they are to increase again in 1989.

Increasing High School Graduation Requirements

In 1983, the Florida legislature mandated increased high school graduation requirements, similar to the university system admission standards of 1981, for all high school graduates. The requirements were to become effective in 1987. By that act, the legislature completed a full circle in the area of mandated graduation requirements since the state's specified standards had been withdrawn some years earlier.

During the discussion about increasing graduation requirements, the concern was expressed that this action might reduce minority enrollment in higher education and cause Florida's already low ranking in secondary school persistence rates between ninth grade and graduation to drop even more. To assist in the transition to college, a series of four instruments was authorized for use in the two-year and four-year institutions for the purpose of guidance and placement. Minimum cutoff scores were set. Students admitted who scored below those levels were required to enroll in a noncredit activity in either communication or computation. The students enrolled in noncredit work would be funded as part of the community college mission, not as part of the university mission. University students so enrolled would normally be instructed by an area community college, sometimes on the university campus by contract arrangement.

What Have Been the Results?

The evidence that accumulated between the 1978–79 and 1984–85 school years shows that the persistence rates from ninth grade through graduation remained constant at 54 percent for black students and that they rose from 57 percent to 64 percent for Hispanic students. While there was an increase in the proportion of blacks who entered postsecondary education in Florida's public institutions between 1978 and 1980, the numbers have leveled off and in some cases declined. The proportion of Hispanics who entered postsecondary education has continued to rise since 1978.

An analysis by Florida Board of Regents staff in 1982 and 1983 showed that the largest cause of the decline in black enrollment in postsecondary education directly from secondary schools was heavy military recruiting that offered options for later education benefits. While the male–female breakout among most racial groups seldom exceeded 54 percent–46 percent, black enrollment in the state university system for entering students was nearly 65 percent female. During the early 1980s, the leveling off of black enrollment in most of the southern states occurred in open-access as well as in selective admissions institutions, both two-year and four-year. Florida's experience with assessment does not seem to have reduced access for minorities.

A review of changes in CLAST scores since the first administration in October 1982 shows that passing rates for blacks increased 38 percentage points to 72.6 percent, Hispanics increased 37 percentage points to 90.4 percent, and whites increased 13 percentage points to 93.1 percent.

At Florida A. & M. University, the state's traditionally black institution that still has a large majority of black students, the June 1986 passing rate on all five subtests of the CLAST was 85.5 percent. This figure can be compared with passing rates of 33 percent in June 1983, 46 percent in June 1984, and 52.2 percent in June 1985. Early in this process, Florida A. & M. focused additional resources and support programs at the lower-division computation and communication levels. The school reports that this investment is paying off in student achievement.

A review of the increased high school graduation requirements showed that in 1983, 63 percent of blacks would meet the 1986 English requirements. By 1985, that proportion had risen to 90 percent. In 1983, 45 percent of blacks would have met the 1986 mathematics requirements. By 1985, that proportion had risen to 87 percent. Similar gains occurred for Hispanic and white students, although they were not as dramatic.

Retention in College

If 1979 is used as the base year for first-time-in-college entering students, the university system is showing improved retention. In the four-year period that ended in 1983, the two-year rate of retention for the largest minority population groups was as follows: Black students improved from 60.2 percent to 73.6 percent, and Hispanic students improved from 70.9 percent to 81.4 percent. Longer-range studies are continuing. It appears that the opportunity for special counseling services and a more regularized advisement program may be as effective in this process as the precollege curriculum experiences.

Engineering: A Target Area

Engineering had the smallest share of minority enrollment, particularly black. As a result of a five-year plan to expand and improve this discipline in Florida, a special commitment was made to counsel and recruit more minorities. Evidence for the 1978–1980 period showed few blacks being counseled into engineering in Florida, either at the high school or college level. Precollege experiences in the math and science areas were often minor.

In fall 1980, 542 blacks were enrolled in engineering programs in the state university system. By fall 1985, that number had risen to 826, a gain of 52.4 percent. In fall 1980, 573 Hispanics were enrolled in engineering programs. By fall 1985, that number had risen to 1,285, a gain of 124.2 percent. These impressive gains were accompanied by a major state commitment for new facilities, equipment, and faculty and by an overall enrollment growth that totaled 55.8 percent for the system in engineering.

Conclusion

One of the concerns that led to Florida's assessment programs was loss of credibility in the link between instruction and credentialing. The analysis thus far of the several components of assessment indicates that quality control and credibility are being restored. Most of the goals of Florida's assessment plan appear to be on target in 1986. High school graduates exit with more college-preparatory course work than they did in the past, and there have been score gains in the past two years among those students on both of the nationally normed college admissions tests. Dramatic gains in college enrollment are occurring for Hispanic students in postsecondary programs, while black enrollment tends to remain fairly level. Retention is up in college programs, CLAST scores show improvement, and target programs, such as engineering, have seen dramatic gains in minority enrollment.

When assessment is used with discretion and good planning, it can be a useful tool to help minorities to succeed in postsecondary education. Of course, while Florida can point with pride to some achievement, much remains to be done. Exemplary programs that have produced results need to be expanded. Changes in policies that have the effect of restricting access, such as changes in financial aid policies, and class schedules that are inconvenient for part-timers may need to be adjusted. Success will come over many years of diligent effort and commitment.

Roy E. McTarnaghan is vice-chancellor of the State University System of Florida.

Rapidly changing technology will have a dramatic impact on assessment of students both for placement and instruction. An exciting potential for increased individualization is available if we but choose to use it.

Technology and Testing: What Is Around the Corner?

Jeanine C. Rounds, Martha J. Kanter, Marlene Blumin

> We are now on the verge of a technological revolution in testing. Paradoxically, the new testing is, in a sense, a return to old-fashioned individualized examinations. . . . Now, however, the arbitrariness and lack of objectivity of such exams will have been removed [Wainer, 1983, p. 16].

Whether this optimistic prediction will become true remains to be seen. However, in recent years, as assessment at college has made a major resurgence, schools are looking increasingly toward technology to help with the process of administering, scoring, and even interpreting the results of assessment activities. As the number of students to be tested has grown and as the level of the information requested has risen, the computer and computer-related technology have become essential components of testing programs. The speed, depth, and breadth of the data that they make available and their ability to synthesize these data with other information that may be available have already ushered in a new period of testing. Along with technological change, advances in the field of cognitive science, particularly in information processing, offer possibilities for new and exciting applications to testing. As a result, testing is being linked to

D. Bray, and M. J. Belcher (eds.). *Issues in Student Assessment.*
New Directions for Community Colleges, no. 59. San Francisco: Jossey-Bass, Fall 1987.

improvement of instruction and to student retention and learning outcomes as well as to initial placement. As the technology continues to improve and as our ability to collect and interpret information increases, we can only hope that the result will in fact be an emphasis on individual qualities.

Many of the capabilities that once seemed to lie in the distant future are now available, and others soon will be. For example, we are becoming remarkably more efficient in data synthesis and analysis. Immediate and individual feedback is available on many campuses. In addition, the computer-adaptive test is already in use at a few locations. Computer-adaptive tests free assessment from the constraints of the timed test that adversely affect many test takers. Diagnosis of individual academic skills is now available, as is analysis of physical skills. Assessment tasks that use simulation or interactive videodiscs are also coming to the market. Such tests will provide more realistic assessment tasks in many areas. Regular measurement of learning outcomes will identify efficient learning modes for individual students and have an impact both on curriculum and on instructional delivery. Yet another impact in the near future will be the use of the computer to analyze relatively subjective areas, such as writing. The opportunities are limitless. The issue of key interest to educators is the use to which the technology will be put.

Pretest Use of Computers

One major way in which computers are currently being used is for test preparation. Software is being developed to prepare students for exams and even to provide simulated versions of the tests. The test preparation software now available includes materials for the high school proficiency (G.E.D.) exam, the Scholastic Aptitude Test (SAT), and the American College Testing Program (ACT) exam. Four years ago, Silverman and Dunn (1983) reviewed ten programs developed just to prepare students for the SAT. In summer 1986, two forms of software to practice the Graduate Management Admission Test (GMAT) became available, one that provided immediate item-by-item feedback and one that simulated the actual test. Practice software for the Graduate Record Examination (GRE) was offered in fall 1986. Ward (1984) notes that one important benefit of such software may be motivational, with students finding it more entertaining to attack review and drill at the computer than on paper. A second value may be utilization of the computer to monitor the student's performance, because the computer can track the student's use of time, branch between practice and instruction, reintroduce questions that prove troublesome, and in short provide considerably more individualization than is usually available in the classroom.

Computer-Adaptive Placement Tests

Tests are also being developed to be taken directly at the computer. The new placement tests are among those of greatest interest. In some instances, traditional tests have simply been transferred to machines, but a more recent development is the computer-adaptive test, which has different questions for different test takers. In such tests, the difficulty level of each succeeding question depends on whether the student answers the previous question correctly. Such a test begins to capitalize on the capabilities available with a computer.

Moving toward extensive use of the computer, Educational Testing Service (ETS) completed the pilot-testing of its computer-adaptive placement battery (Computerized Placement Test) in 1986 and subsequently made the test available for purchase. The three modules offered include written communication, learning skills, and mathematics. The student takes the test at the computer, responding to questions through an easily learned response mode. If the student's answer is correct, the computer provides a more difficult question. If the student's answer is incorrect, the computer asks an easier question, thus testing at the student's instructional rather than at the student's frustration level. This format, which makes use of a data bank of 120 questions for each test area, requires each student to answer between twelve and seventeen questions before the student's ability level can be determined with accuracy (Forehand, 1986).

ACT is also offering computerized assessment. It is designing new components for its computer-adaptive testing, and it has plans to link skills testing with its vocational assessment and career-planning package, Discover. A pilot study is under way at Phoenix College in Maricopa District, Arizona, where 100 computer terminals are being used for college entrance testing (Papparella, 1986).

Adaptive testing requires a large item bank; each item must be scaled according to its difficulty. The computer stores the items, calculates their selection, and facilitates test administration. Adaptive testing is made possible by an advance in measurement theory known as *item response theory*, which provides a mathematical basis for selection of the appropriate question at each point and for computation of scores that are compatible between individuals. Item response theory has been the subject of intensive theoretical and empirical research for thirty years, but its demanding computational requirements have prevented it from being feasible for use in microcomputer testing until recently (Lord, 1980).

Traditional norm-referenced testing usually offers a large number of moderately difficult questions with a few very easy questions and a few very difficult questions. In order to discriminate ability levels, everyone who is tested is asked to answer all the questions. Computer-adaptive testing can obtain the same results by asking only a few questions. However, such testing requires extensive research and data to develop the question pool and the computational procedures. These are available only in powerful computers (including some microcomputers), so the most effective use will probably continue to be for professionally developed large-scale placement and diagnostic tests.

According to Wainer (1983), computer-adaptive testing has the following advantages: Test security is improved; the individual can work at his or her own pace, and the speed with which the individual responds provides additional assessment information; each examinee stays productive, challenged but not discouraged; there are no problems with answer sheets, erasures, or response ambiguity; the test can be scored immediately; and immediate feedback is available in the form of various reports.

The fact that the test is not timed is another benefit, since it takes the pressure off test-anxious or handicapped students. In addition, it minimizes the need for monitoring. Still another advantage is the flexibility that it affords: Students can be tested at virtually any time; students who register late or otherwise miss mass testing dates and students who need test results at a particular moment can be quickly served. Such a test also provides an alternative for students who want to challenge the results of other tests.

In addition, according to one school involved in the pilot-testing for ETS, students are surprisingly positive about taking the test on the computer, even those who have never used a computer before. The testing officer admitted that he had been reluctant to use the computer-adaptive test but that he was now enthusiastic because of its versatility and because of the very positive student response (Rutledge, 1986).

The disadvantages of computer-adaptive testing include the necessity of providing every test taker with a computer terminal (thus far, the test can be used only on IBM-compatible machines) and the cost of the test. As terminals proliferate on campuses, the first problem may become less significant, and the costs may be absorbed on many campuses through student fees. Nevertheless, it seems unlikely that the computer-adaptive test will soon completely replace the paper-and-pencil mass testing now in place at most colleges.

Tests Taken at the Computer: Other Types

Many other kinds of tests are being developed for the computer, including academic and vocational assessments and tests for special populations.

Vocational Tests. One area of growing interest is in the field of vocational assessment, both interest and aptitude. A computerized version of the Ohio Vocational Interest Survey (OVIS II) is available. The primary advantage is administrative: With computers, the scores are obtained faster, the speed and accuracy of administration is greatly enhanced, the results are available more quickly, and test security is increased (Hambleton, 1984).

Other tests provide a range of assistance directly to the student. For example, such tests as MicroSkills and Sigi Plus begin with self-analysis questions and permit the student to narrow the focus down so that very specific information can be obtained directly from the computer. MicroSkills asks the student to identify the skills that he or she most wants to continue to use and provides a list of the occupations and industries that best match the student's interests. Sigi Plus integrates the skills, interests, and values that the student has identified into job recommendations.

MESA and Apticom, two vocational batteries, measure both academic and manual skills as well as interests. Students use a joystick to take the MESA test, and the facility with which they use it becomes part of their dexterity measure. Apticom makes use of a "probe" that the student inserts into answer spots on a large card. The data that are recorded include an assessment of eye, hand, and foot coordination and other physical abilities based on speed and accuracy. These skills, along with the student's recorded preferences and answers to math and language questions, are combined into a comprehensive report that makes recommendations, using the *Dictionary of Occupational Titles*, about the vocational choices that seem appropriate.

These tools are coming into increasing use at community colleges, where students, including returning adults, are often confused and unconfident about their own abilities and appropriate career choices.

Special Population Tests. For some students, computers offer a tremendous advantage over paper-and-pencil tests. Large-print systems make the computer screen accessible for individuals with poor vision. Sophisticated screen-reading software, combined with high-level speech synthesizers, such as DECtalk, provides computer access for blind individuals. Questions and responses can be presented through headphones, and the student can hear what he or she has typed on the screen. Students with mild to profound orthopedic disabilities can access the computer through a variety of adaptations, including smart word processors, speech recognition systems, and programs to modify keyboard functions. Spelling checkers, combined with smart word processors and speech output devices, create a new and effective writing environment for students with learning disabilities. A variety of modalities can be used to offer input through visual channels, auditory channels, or both. Other features of computerized testing, including enlarged print, auditory feedback, word-by-word reading and review, varying screen colors, and expanded time frames, have benefits for learning-disabled students.

Diagnostic Assessment and Instruction

Diagnostic assessment, which can be used after initial assessment both as a progress measure and as an outcome measure, is another area of rapidly growing interest.

Diagnostic-prescriptive computer-adaptive test series are currently under development by ETS and ACT (Forehand, 1986; Papparella, 1986). These tests are intended primarily for the classroom or for learning centers after the student has been initially screened. For example, a student may fail the English placement test, but with what specifically is the student having problems? Would it help for a teacher in a remedial math class to know the specific areas in which each student was weak or to have a class profile of students' strengths and weaknesses? Would it help a student who was doing poorly in school to assess his or her study skills?

Both ETS and ACT are betting that the answer is yes to all these questions. At ETS, thirty prototype tests currently under development cover basic and advanced math, grammar, writing, reading, and study skills. Each test is highly interactive. Features include computer-generated narrative reports, feedback and second try when appropriate, special-purpose response modes, an analysis of why mistakes were made (based on the branching that probes beneath the correctness or incorrectness of responses), and instructional suggestions. Although the tests were conceptualized for use at the community college level, interest in the materials is high among those who have worked with them, including professionals from both the high school and the university levels. Seventy-one percent of the students who took part in the field-testing indicated that they preferred to take a test by computer, while only 16 percent indicated no preference (Forehand, 1986).

Linking Assessment and Instruction

Computer technology has increased our ability to draw assessment and instruction activities close together. Research and increasing knowledge about cognitive processes, combined with diagnostic assessment, will have a major impact on instruction. For example, studies to examine the use of language in the cognitive process (Chaffee, 1985) and the student's cognitive approach to a discipline (Chi, Feltovich, and Glaser, 1981; Sternberg, 1981) have been undertaken. These efforts to examine the cognitive process help us to understand the interaction between examinee and machine and the strategies that a learner uses to acquire knowledge. Additional research, in cognitive science in particular, will be valuable for increasing the interrelationship between assessment and instruction (Glaser, 1985; Hunt, 1985; Madaus, 1985).

The future may well see extensive classroom use of the computer diagnostic test, with the interactive computer maintaining a record of every student's performance and tracking errors to identify patterns and problems. On-screen feedback will be immediate, acknowledging correct answers and rectifying incorrect answers or suggesting instructional materials that can correct the errors. As Ward (1984, p. 18) comments, "Identification of errors with this level of precision offers the possibility of specific remediation, and the statement of error leads directly to a prescription for the necessary instruction. . . . These types of analysis may eventually lead to a new generation of assessment instruments that can be linked more directly to instructional sequences than are present tests. Because of the complexity of the models and the application to the analysis of a given student's performance, the computer will be an indispensable tool."

The use of assessment for outcome measurement was the subject of an August 1986 symposium in Laguna Beach, California. Participants—college practitioners from various states—agreed that assessment will become increasingly differentiated in terms of the concepts and capabilities assessed and that it will continue to expand as one product of student consumerism. Participants agreed that such assessment has a formative function and that it should have an impact on curriculum and programs rather than serve as a gate that keeps students from progressing (Bray, 1986). Again, the questions of cost and computer availability may be significant.

Scoring Tests and Generating Data

One other key area in which technology is moving quickly is in scoring tests and sorting data. In the past, technology has been most often tied to the speed of scoring, with machines used to sort, analyze, and even comment on the results. The Scantron machine, which "reads" the pencil marks on special multiple-choice answer sheets fed into the machine and indicates which marks are incorrect, is readily available to many classroom teachers.

However, by linking the machine directly to a computer, institutions have become able to tie machine scoring to a number of other uses. As placement tests are scored by Scantron, the results can be evaluated and entered directly into the students' files, which substantially reduces the time needed for entering data and correcting errors. When necessary, the computer can provide the student, the institution, or both with an immediate printout of the analysis. Typical of the new programs is the software now available through a group of educators in Santa Barbara, California (Computerized Assessment and Placement Programs or CAPP), which links with Scantron and scores the selected test; determines placement; generates reports for counselors, teachers, students, and administrators; and prints an individualized letter and mailing label for each student (Brady and Elmore, 1986).

Major testing companies, such as American College Testing, CTB McGraw–Hill, Educational Testing Service, and the College Board, also offer services that score entrance and placement exams, relate the data to information about other students who have taken the test on a particular campus or to national norms, and provide comprehensive feedback in the form of scores, interpretations, and predictions related to specific programs. Validity studies and data analysis by ethnicity, age, sex, and a host of other variables are becoming increasingly routine. Data available from the companies just named have become increasingly detailed as the companies have competed to meet the assessment needs of college admissions and placement programs.

For example, ASSET, ACT's program for community colleges, incorporates a comprehensive orientation, testing, and research package. The research provides accountability, placement, and retention information and includes an ability profile report for students in specific programs as well as a grade experience table that correlates test results to course grades so that a college can develop its own local placement norms. ACT has recently added software to ASSET.

The Placement Research Service (PRS) offered by the College Board allows an institution to select up to nine different predictors: Seven different tests, two optional predictors (such as high school grades, teacher recommendations, and so forth), and seven different measures of academic success (such as grade point average, grades in English classes, grades in math classes, and faculty ratings) are available. The data provided to the institution include the score distributions, correlations of all predictors, two-way tables of observed data, and expectancy tables.

Information for Students

One impact of the growing emphasis on assessment and information collection has been a movement toward providing students with increasingly complete information, a sort of consumer awareness movement that is a far remove from the days when students' results were a carefully guarded secret held close to the chest by counselors while they gave students the benefit of their professional analysis.

Increasingly, colleges with sophisticated computer systems are developing their own institution-specific programs that report test results directly to the student, providing scores, statistical interpretations, and commentary or advice in different degrees of formality or friendliness. A 1983 study of the four California community college assessment programs that were considered most effective by their colleagues found that one of the few commonalities among the four was the prescriptive computer printout that students were given. Comments ranged from a fairly impersonal listing of scores and recommended classes to a chatty form that addressed the students by their first names and made various suggestions, such as dropping in and visiting a specific person in a tutorial program (Rounds, 1983). Such reports are given to students individually or in group settings where college staff review particular responses and help students with further interpretation. The reports are considered cost-effective, and they can be used to supplement or even replace individual meetings with counselors.

There is also a growing interest in "expectancy" or "probability" tables, such as those provided by both ACT and ETS. Using correlation data from previous test scores and grades, such tables estimate the probability that a student with a specific score has of earning a specific grade in an identified course. Many counselors consider such a table to be an effective way of guiding student selection.

The Future

Many exciting possibilities for the use of computers are already being explored, and others lie just around the corner. Test capabilities include options that should provide us with a better way of assessing each individual. For example, a wider variety of questions is becoming possible—including memory testing through successive frames, and, with voice synthesizers, spelling tests and tests of the understanding of spoken language.

Advances in technology permit the increased use of graphics and animation to simulate the actions and events that are the focus of a question. Simulations that permit students to select activities and solutions—that simulate a chemistry experiment or a nursing problem, for example—may be a better way of assessing some skills than the ways we now possess. Simulations could replace the long written narratives describing problem-solving situations on exams for police and fire fighters. The use of interactive video will open many additional options, including touch screens for item response. For example, ACT already has experiments under way linking videodisc technology with the Discover career-planning package to offer real-life presentations to students. Improvements in optical disc technology should soon make desktop storage of high-resolution visual displays an inexpensive and convenient way of presenting test stimuli (Millman, 1984; Hale, Oakey, Shaw, and Burns, 1985; Ziegler, 1986).

Another exciting possibility may be analysis of student writing. Although such analysis currently seems beyond the range of computers, such systems as Bell's Writer's Workbench, IBM's Epistle, and UCLA's WANDA program have already made substantial progress in analysis of writing samples. All these systems are able to detect a number of errors and writing weaknesses and to measure low-order writing attributes. Perhaps it is not too much to hope that one day the computer may be able to handle the student essay.

As we gain better information about cognitive processes and as the speed and efficiency of computer technology increase, we should be able to develop measures that test each individual's special skills and knowledge and provide the diagnostic information that will be most useful in helping students to make effective choices. Ongoing diagnosis will affect selection of learning tasks and classroom instruction. Accuracy and speed will improve, and costs should decrease as we capitalize on the special opportunities provided by the computer.

The possibilities are limitless and exciting. If we are able to maintain humanistic goals for assessment, then perhaps Wainer's (1983) optimism will be vindicated. The focus will be on the qualities of the individual, and technology will be a wise servant, not a demanding master.

References

Brady, G., and Elmore, R. Personal communication, November 1986.

Bray, D. "Report of Symposium on College Outcomes Assessment." Unpublished report, Laguna Beach, Calif., 1986.

Chaffee, J. "Viewing Reading and Writing as Thinking Processes." Paper presented at the 69th annual meeting of the American Educational Research Association, Chicago, 1985.

Chi, J., Feltovich, P. J., and Glaser, R. "Categorization and Representation of Physics Problems by Experts and Novices." *Cognitive Science*, 1981, 5 (2), 121–152.

Forehand, G. *Research Memorandum: Computerized Diagnostic Testing.* Princeton, N.J.: Educational Testing Service, 1986.

Glaser, R. "The Integration of Instruction and Testing." Paper presented at the Educational Testing Service Invitational Conference, New York, 1985.

Hale, M. E., Oakey, J. R., Shaw, E. L., and Burns, J. "Using Computer Animation in Science Testing." *Computers in the Schools*, 1985, 2 (1), 83–90.

Hambleton, R. K. "Using Microcomputers to Develop Tests." *Educational Measurement: Issues and Practice*, 1984, 3 (2), 10–14.

Hunt, E. "Cognitive Research and Future Test Design." Paper presented at the Educational Testing Service Invitational Conference, New York, 1985.

Lord, F. M. *Application of Item Response Theory to Practical Testing Problems.* Hillsdale, N.J.: Erlbaum, 1980.

Madaus, G. "The Perils and Promises of New Tests and New Technologies: Dick and Jane and the Great Analytical Engine." Paper presented at the Educational Testing Service Invitational Conference, New York, 1985.

Millman, J. "Using Microcomputers to Administer Tests: An Alternative Point of View." *Educational Measurement: Issues and Practice*, 1984, 3 (2), 20–21.

Papparella, M. Personal communication, Sacramento, Calif., November 1986.

Rounds, J. C. "Admissions, Placement, and Competency: Assessment Practices in California Community Colleges, 1982-1983." Unpublished doctoral disseration, Brigham Young University, 1983.

Rutledge, R. Personal communication, November 1986.

Silverman, S., and Dunn, S. "Raising SAT Scores: How One School Did It." *Electronic Learning*, 1983, 2 (7), 51–53.

Sternberg, R. J. "Intelligence and Nonentrenchment." *Journal of Educational Psychology*, 1981, 73 (1), 1–16.

Wainer, H. "On Item Response Theory and Computerized Adaptive Tests." *Journal of College Admissions*, 1983, *28* (4), 9–16.

Ward, W. "Using Microcomputers to Administer Tests." *Educational Measurement: Issues and Practices*, 1984, *3* (2), 16–20.

Ziegler, T. "Learning Technology with the Interactive Videodisc." *Journal of Studies in Technical Careers*, 1986, *8* (1), 53–60.

Jeanine C. Rounds is associate dean of instructional services at Yuba College, California, where she is in charge of district grants and off-campus classes in a three-county area.

Martha J. Kanter is director of support services for Monterey Peninsula College in Monterey, California and president of the Learning Assessment Retention Consortium of California.

Marlene Blumin is professor of reading and coordinator of basic skills at Tompkins Cortland Community College in Dryden, New York.

Assessment systems need to be designed for new student populations—the "new" majority who no longer fit the traditional profile. In contrast to programs for full-time students who are recent high school graduates, the model proposed here features a customized planning information sequence tailored to the diversity of today's students.

Is There Life After College? A Customized Assessment and Planning Model

Susan S. Obler, Maureen H. Ramer

Maria is twenty-five years old, entering college for the first time after a series of secretarial jobs following high school graduation. She longs for more stimulating work, having discovered that she is more skilled with subordinates than her supervisors are. However, she suspects that she will need a college degree in order to move forward into more challenging positions.

George has entered college directly from high school, where he just barely accumulated enough credits to graduate. With his buddies, he shares a vague sense that "college is good for you," but they have very amorphous goals. They also have little family support for delaying full-time employment.

Sherril is thirty-two years old and recently divorced. She has two boys, ages three and nine. Although she is very motivated to find fulfilling work, she fears that her basic skills will not permit her to compete in the job market. She favors the health care field, but she wonders where her talents will fit.

Nguyen, a former teacher, is forty years old. He has been in this country for two years. His language skills are improving, but his factory

D. Bray, and M. J. Belcher (eds.). *Issues in Student Assessment.*
New Directions for Community Colleges, no. 59. San Francisco: Jossey-Bass, Fall 1987.

job wastes his many skills, and his low career status is disturbing at best. His employer is closing the plant, and Nguyen's technical skills will need updating if he is to remain in manufacturing. Understandably, he would love to return to teaching.

These and a large percentage of community college students today no longer fit the traditional profile of the recent high school graduate who plans to get an A.A. or B.A. Many assessment and matriculation programs are designed for the traditional student. In contrast, today's "new" students need an individualized career assessment and guidance process that provides them with the information and interaction that they need in order to plan intelligently.

In spite of the numerous reports on new student populations, there is a gap between the awareness of these changes and existing campus

Figure 1. Assessment and Counseling Paradigms

Previous Emphases: Traditional Community College Student	*Emerging Emphases:* New Community College Student
High-school or G.E.D. graduate; first-career oriented	Adult student; first career and career redirection
Curriculum planning: "Major," short-range planning, or transfer	Curriculum planning: long-range career development, professional paths
School or college as end in itself	College training as means to goal
Youth-oriented guidance counseling staff	Adult-oriented career assessment staff
School role: internal review of available programs based on limited information	College role: external review of planning and decision making based on expanded information
Community college role over when student transfers or completes A.A. or certificate	Community college role continues to assist in recurring career decisions
Present-oriented, short-range, one-job, narrow skills focus	Future-oriented, cross-career skills, focus emphasizing problem solving, communication, critical thinking
Assessment: narrow, skills and achievement oriented	Assessment: broad, value added, and potential oriented
Curriculum designed as foundation for further academic study (organization centered)	Curriculum designed to provide adults with workplace skills and growth (student centered)
Assessment occurs once only as a review before registration or as an orientation process	Initial assessment forms baseline used to monitor subsequent progress; follow-up occurs regularly
All students follow same assessment process	Customized process focuses on individual students

assessment programs. The lack of appropriate services continues to stymie student success. Most of the new students are adults, and the goals of many are vague. At the same time, college personnel have scrambled to survive menacing budget cuts and declining enrollment. Their energies have been distracted from the assessment needs of these new students, and funding for new programs has been extremely limited. The expanded assessment model proposed here is consistent with the emerging paradigm that emphasizes the "new" adult student.

Shifting Paradigms: From Prescribing to Empowering

Due to the history of the community college movement, assessment and counseling services were once modeled after secondary school approaches. The goals of assessment and guidance were somewhat binary: college or noncollege, transfer or nontransfer. Students were then advised on class schedules for available curricula. With such a narrow focus, assessment serves the college programs more than it does the students, and the curriculum becomes an end in itself rather than the means to a goal (Garza, 1986). Such goal displacement and constricted options can threaten students' motivation. That is, if assessment systems communicate limited, short-range purposes, students will perceive assessment in the same dead-end way.

These changes in perception and approach appear as paradigm shifts in Figure 1. The old, narrow system designed for the traditional student is moving toward a broad, diversified model that serves the needs of the new student.

The Assessment Model in Action

The broad assessment model proposed here—it is depicted in Figure 2—is based on four assertions: First, students will succeed more readily with clear goals. Second, most students intend to pursue a career after college. Third, many adults require help with career redirection. Fourth, community colleges should be the primary community resource for career redirection. The goal of this model is to enable students to define their personal goals and to plan an instructional program as quickly as possible.

Every student begins with an interview that is conducted by a professional career counselor. The counselor obtains a profile of the student's formal education (A). If the student has a defined career goal, he or she will only require assessment of the basic skill competencies directly related to the objective. The student then proceeds to step (F) in order to develop an academic plan. However, most practitioners recognize that students who do not have a clearly defined career goal need to proceed through several steps in the process.

Figure 2. Model for Career Assessment and Educational Planning

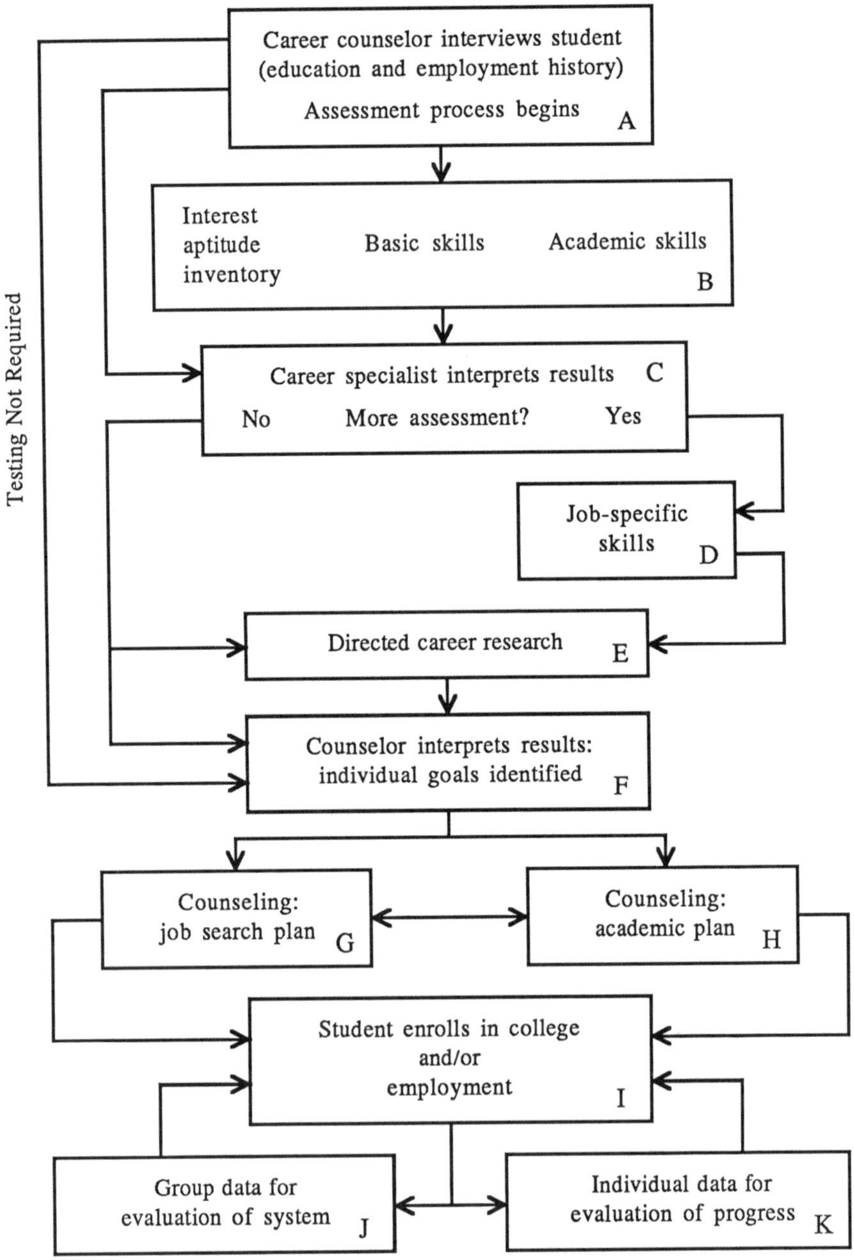

For example, Maria needs only part of the model due to her work history. Following the intake interview, she receives a plan for tests in career aptitude and personality and interest inventories for professional level positions (B). She and the career specialist consider and interpret the results (C). She finds that she is detail oriented and well suited to fiscal management careers. She agrees with the outcome of the testing, so she does not need the directed career research (E). With her counselor, she develops an academic plan (H): an A.A. degree in accounting with electives in business management. She enrolls in college (I).

George discusses his limited high school record at the initial interview (A). Since he has little work experience, he and his counselor decide that he should take the full range of tests: basic skills, career testing, aptitude, and so on (B). At the test results interview (C), George's interest in art emerges undeniably. Following additional tests (D) to determine his occupational focus, he conducts directed career research (E) on the requirements in the various commercial art fields. With these data, George reviews his alternatives in another interview (F), and he decides to enter commercial art. Unfortunately, his college does not have this program, so he is referred to a neighboring college that does.

Sherril discusses her lack of confidence in communication skills and receives a plan for basic skills tests, interest inventories related to the health care field, and aptitude testing (B). After these tests, she meets with the career counselor to review her results (C). Her test results indicate a strong interest in the field of respiratory therapy. To find out more, she pursues directed career research (E). After reviewing all her information with a counselor (F), she develops an academic plan (H) and enrolls in college (I).

At his intake interview, Nguyen discusses his desire to return to the teaching he loved in his native land. Since his goal is clearly defined, his tests are primarily limited to academic skills (B). After the career specialist interprets his results (C), Nguyen conducts career research to determine the requirements for a teaching credential in the state (E). The information is reviewed (F), and the curriculum plan that is developed (H) includes written and oral language skills and the lower-division course work required for a teaching credential.

The means for gathering data that can be used to evaluate the progress both of individuals and of groups is built into this system. One of the goals of the process is to retain students by helping them to define their goals. The individual data and subsequent evaluation (K) are the means for measuring the success of this outcome. The overall group data and subsequent evaluation (J) are a means of measuring the success of the system to increase the retention of students.

The Strength of the Model

The model described here has many strengths and advantages. First, the assessment and interpretation procedures are completely customized to each student; this feature communicates the college's willingness to deal with the needs and abilities of individuals. Further, the student's personal involvement helps the student to "own" his or her goals and increases the student's motivation. The student also has a full report and discussion of his or her strengths and liabilities. Because the student and the counselor are in contact at every step, the evolving exchange incorporates old data into new.

Another advantage of this model is the documented and professionally reviewed educational plan that the student receives. The spiral of activities permits student and counselor to expand data and readdress goals as often as needed. These branched steps provide the time and the information needed for planning the most direct route to the student's goal. The more direct the student's route to his or her goals, the more the student's persistence increases.

Admittedly, the thorough, customized process envisioned in this model requires careful planning and budgeting. Yet, on balance, the program could save the college revenue that is ordinarily lost through the attrition of students who have ambiguous goals. One way of generating funds for this kind of assessment system is to offer it as a variable-unit, open-entry "course." Colleges could also use the resources in federally funded job training and vocational education programs for this purpose. At the least, external funding could offset the start-up costs for tests and personnel. Further, colleges could charge fees to nonenrollees from the community.

Thus, the model helps colleges to fill the perilous gaps between test results and a student's future. As Loacker, Cromwell, and O'Brien (1986, p. 48) have written, "Testing, as it is frequently practiced, can tell us how much and what kind of knowledge someone possesses, whereas assessment provides a basis for inferring what the person can do with that knowledge . . . Assessment aims to elicit a demonstration of the nature, extent, and quality of his or her ability in action." It is in this broader spirit of assessment, not in the narrow use of testing, that the model described here can empower the nontraditional student. Colleges must once again focus their mission on the student's future and provide the powerful information needed to realize and improve life after college.

References

Garza, P. C., Jr. "A Student-Centered Professional Career Advising System." Unpublished paper, Rio Hondo College, 1986.

Loacker, G., Cromwell, L., and O'Brien, K. "Assessment in Higher Education: To Serve the Learner." In C. Adelman (ed.), *Assessment in Higher Education: Issues and Contexts.* Washington, D.C.: Office of Educational Research and Improvement, U.S. Department of Education, 1986.

Susan S. Obler is instructor of composition and coordinator of English placement at Rio Hondo College in Whittier, California.

Maureen H. Ramer is dean of occupational education at Rio Hondo College in Whittier, California.

*Materials abstracted from recent additions to the Educational
Resources Information Center (ERIC) system provide further
information on student assessment at community colleges.*

Sources and Information: Student Assessment at Community Colleges

Jim Palmer

Student assessment and placement programs pose several educational and logistical problems for community college administrators: Who should be assessed and when? What tests should be used, and how will cutoff scores be determined? Should remediation be mandatory for those whose test scores fall below the cutoff point. How does the testing program complement other student services, such as advising and counseling? These questions are addressed in a growing body of literature on assessment practices at two-year colleges. Selections from this literature reviewed here include descriptions of institutional assessment programs, college efforts to evaluate testing programs and assess the predictive validity of testing instruments, state initiatives in testing (with particular emphasis on Florida's College-Level Academic Skills Test), and the use of cohort testing to assess curricular efficacy.

Descriptions of Testing Programs

During the early 1980s, growing interest in student assessment led researchers to survey assessment and placement practices at community

D. Bray, and M. J. Belcher (eds.). *Issues in Student Assessment.*
New Directions for Community Colleges, no. 59. San Francisco: Jossey-Bass, Fall 1987.

colleges. The resulting literature includes descriptions of institutional assessment programs at Sacramento City College in California (Haase and Caffrey, 1983), the Grossmont Community College District in California (Wiener, 1984–85), and Triton College in Illinois (Chand, 1985). A number of statewide analyses have appeared, including Ramey (1981), who examines the procedures used by Florida community colleges in 1980 to assess the skills of entering students; Rivera (1981a, 1981b), who describes English placement systems at community colleges in California and Arizona; Forstall (1984), who reviews the approaches to student assessment and placement used by the Illinois community colleges; Rounds (1984) and Rounds and Andersen (1984), who examine placement practices in the California community colleges; and the Washington State Student Services Commission (1985), which outlines the components of model assessment programs in place at the Washington community colleges. The information in these reports cannot be considered current, because practices in the area of assessment and placement change continuously. Nonetheless, they point to the diversity of assessment practices employed and emphasize that the colleges differ greatly in terms of the subject areas assessed, the assessment instruments used, and the ways in which the results of assessment are used to advise and place students. A composite picture of community college assessment practices is not easy to draw.

Most of the studies just named show that assessment efforts serve primarily as a sorting function for entering students. While this function serves the useful purpose of identifying students whose skills deficiencies jeopardize their chances of completing college-level courses successfully, some authors have pointed out that assessment information is more effectively used in the context of student flow. For example, Walvekar (1982) urges a three-stage approach to evaluation: assessment of skills at entrance, ongoing assessment of students during their college career to determine whether instructional programs need to be modified in order to meet student needs, and follow-up evaluation to document student learning on program or course completion. Cohen (1984–85) argues that assessment should be viewed as part of an overall student retention effort, not simply as an initial placement mechanism. He draws on the literature to show how student orientation, tutorial activities, and other supplemental support services complement entry testing in an overall retention program that starts with recruitment and ends with follow-up activities. Finally, Bray (1986) urges educators to link assessment outcomes with instructional improvement and student retention by using test results as a guide to course development and student services. She illustrates how this can be done by describing the student flow model at Sacramento City College (California) and the assessment and placement model developed by the Learning, Assessment, and Retention Consortium of the California community colleges.

Evaluating Student Assessment Programs

Do assessment and placement programs improve student academic performance and persistence? A few colleges have used quasi-experimental designs to assess the academic performance of students who followed the placement prescriptions generated by assessment procedures. The results are mixed, reflecting the difficulty of drawing causal relationships between assessment and academic performance.

Among those attributing positive effects to student assessment are Boggs (1984), Borst and Cordrey (1984), and Richards (1986). Boggs (1984) compares the overall grade point average (GPA) of students in English classes at Butte College (California) before and after implementation of the college's literacy skills assessment program. He determined that, while the high school GPAs of entering students did not significantly change after implementation of the assessment program, the college GPAs of the students did. Borst and Cordrey (1984) compare the cumulative GPAs earned over three semesters by two groups of students at Fullerton College (California): those who tested poorly in reading or writing skills and subsequently underwent remediation and those who tested poorly but avoided placement in remedial classes. The students undergoing remediation earned higher GPAs, which led the authors to suggest that the chances of academic success increase if students follow assessment prescriptions. Richards (1986) conducted a similar analysis, comparing the academic success and persistence of Colorado community college students who followed assessment prescriptions regarding course placement with the success and persistence of those who did not. The former tended to succeed at a significantly higher rate than the latter, but in a small number of cases those who did not follow the advice of counselors succeeded nonetheless.

Losak and Morris (1983) have also documented the phenomenon of successful students who do not follow placement prescriptions. They suggest that a student's deliberate decision not to enroll in remedial courses despite poor test scores may in some cases be appropriate. The authors base this position on an examination of the retention and graduation rates of students who entered Miami–Dade Community College (Florida) in fall 1980. More than half of the entrants whose basic skills test scores indicated a need for remediation chose not to participate in remedial classes. It is interesting that the retention and graduation rates of these students were as high as or higher than the retention and graduation rates of students who did take remedial classes.

Friedlander's (1984) evaluation of the Student Orientation, Assessment, Advisement, and Retention program (SOAAR) at Napa Valley College (California) also suggests that assessment and placement services may not always be effective. SOAAR was designed to assess entering students' reading skills, advise students with low assessment scores to enroll in remedial courses, and inform students of college services. But, Friedlander compared SOAAR students to a similar group of students enrolled before implementation of the SOAAR program and found the SOAAR students were actually less likely to complete courses and earn passing grades. He also found that test scores did not predict student success accurately and that SOAAR did not increase students' use of supplemental support services. Among other recommendations, Friedlander (1984, p. 4) proposes that "assessment of students' skills should go beyond reading and arithmetic ability to include study skills and, if possible, attitude toward learning."

Assessment Validity

The literature is also concerned with the predictive validity of the testing instruments used in assessment programs. Several documents describe college efforts to correlate subsequent student grades with scores on various tests, including the Differential Aptitude Tests (Digby, 1986); the College Board's Descriptive Tests of Language Skills (Rasor and Powell, 1984); the American College Testing Program's Assessment of Student Skills for Entry and Transfer (Abbott, 1986; Santa Rosa Junior College, 1984; Roberts, 1986); the College Board's Multiple Assessment Programs and Services (Abbott, 1986); the English Qualifying Exam (Beavers, 1983); the Nelson Denny Reading Tests (Loucks, 1985); and the Comparative Guidance and Placement Program's tests of reading and written English expression (Miami–Dade Community College, 1985). Most of these studies find only low correlations, if any, between test scores at entrance and subsequent student grades, reflecting the fact that variances in instructor grading practices make it difficult to predict grade outcomes uniformly. For example, Spahr (1983) regressed the English and algebra grades earned by students at Morton College (Illinois) against several independent variables and determined that, while placement test scores accounted for about 15 percent of the variance in student grades, instructor differences accounted for about 27 percent.

Thus, the weight of the evidence shows that the predictive validity of entrance tests in terms of subsequent grades is highly questionable. In light of this, several authors urge that tests be used with caution. For example, Spahr (1983) argues that assessment programs must consider the multiple factors that affect academic success in addition to cognitive ability in specific skills. This may require colleges, he concludes, to use multiple cutoff scores, eliminate entrance testing altogether for certain programs, or work with faculty to minimize inconsistencies in grading practices. Neault (1984) concurs that there is a need for the cautious application of testing and urges colleges to eschew rigid adherence to absolute cutoff scores in recognition of the fact that many students are borderline cases.

State Testing Initiatives

In addition to the application in student placement, states also use testing as an accountability tool certifying that the students who advance through the educational pipeline have mastered reading, writing, and computational skills. For example, New Jersey requires entering students in the state's public postsecondary institutions to take the New Jersey College Basic Skills Placement Test; test results are used to place students needing remediation and to monitor changes in the skills abilities of entering students over time (New Jersey Basic Skills Council, 1986). In Georgia, the Board of Regents of the state university system requires degree-seeking students in public colleges and universities to demonstrate minimum competencies in reading and writing skills (Bridges, 1986).

Much of the literature on state-mandated minimum competency testing focuses on the tests required for high school graduation or for those seeking teacher certification. But, Florida's College-Level Academic Skills Test (CLAST), which is required of all students seeking an associate in arts degree or upper-division status in the state university system, has placed the issue of minimum competency testing squarely within the realm of the community college transfer function: Students must pass the test in order to attain junior status. Much of the literature on CLAST emanates from the Office of Institutional Research at Miami–Dade Community College. Drawing on the CLAST scores of Miami–Dade students, these reports focus on such topics as the characteristics and educational backgrounds of students who fail (Belcher, 1984b, 1986); CLAST outcomes for special populations, including those who enter the community college with test scores that make them ineligible for the state university system (Losak, 1984b; Belcher and Losak, 1985), ethnic minorities (Belcher, 1984c), and English-as-a-second-language students (Belcher, 1985e); the relationship between grades earned at Miami–Dade and subsequent performance on the CLAST (Belcher, 1985a; Losak, 1984a); the relationship between a student's level of basic skills at entry and pass-fail rate on the CLAST (Belcher, 1984a); the curricular correlates of success on CLAST, including the contribution of developmental, mathematics, and English classes to student pass rates (Belcher, 1985b, 1985c, 1985f); the effect of increased test-taking time on CLAST performance (Wright, 1984a); the question of whether additional attention to test-taking strategies might significantly improve passing rates (Belcher, 1985d); and students' opinions on the adequacy of their preparation for the CLAST (Wright, 1984b). These reports reveal that those entering the college with lower skill levels tend to have a more difficult time passing the CLAST exams. In comparison to those who pass all four sections, students who fail were more likely to have been in the bottom of the percentile on entrance tests, to have listed a language other than English as their first language, to have higher course withdrawal rates, and to earn lower grade point averages. Nonetheless, Losak (1984a) points to an imperfect relation between academic success and CLAST performance, noting that 20 percent of the associate degree graduates who took the CLAST in fall 1983 failed one or more of the CLAST subcomponents. He concludes that student grades may not necessarily reflect the competencies requisite to successful competition on the CLAST.

Cohort Testing

While such tests as the CLAST may satisfy the political need to certify student competency in basic skills, some scholars point out that they cannot account for the aggregate of what students learn in college courses. For example, Cohen and Brawer (1987) argue that tests required of students who move from one grade level to another focus only on the most rudimentary skills and drive students toward classes in the basics, away from more specialized courses in the arts and sciences. A better approach to accountability, Cohen and Brawer argue, is to require criterion-referenced tests in the liberal arts to be taken periodically by cohorts of students as they progress through college. While such tests cannot be used to place students in classes or to make decisions about individuals, they can be used to measure the value added to student cohorts as a whole from year to year. Thus, cohort testing turns the focus of the college assessment program from placing students to estimating the efficacy of curriculum and instruction as a whole.

As an example of cohort testing, Cohen and Brawer (1987) describe the General Academic Assessment (GAA) and its administration to 8,026 students at four large urban community college districts in 1984. The GAA is a test of student knowledge in the liberal arts and includes representative items in the humanities, sciences, social sciences, mathematics, and English usage. Cohen and Brawer determined that there was a direct relationship between GAA scores and the number of units completed by students; for example, the more humanities courses a student had taken, the higher the student's score on the humanities section of the GAA. If appropriate controls were introduced, Cohen and Brawer argue, colleges could use such tests as the GAA in multiple-matrix programs to gain information on student learning and program outcomes that could be sent to state agencies. Riley (1984) provides further information on the GAA.

Conclusion

This concluding chapter has reviewed the recent literature on student assessment at the community college. Several themes emerge: descriptive analyses of testing and assessment programs, the problem of incorporating student assessment into ongoing student flow and retention programs, the limited predictive validity of placement tests, the use of minimum competency testing as an accountability measure, and the alternative use of cohort testing to document student learning. The publications cited here by no means constitute the entire body of the student literature on student assessment. Additional writings can be found through manual or computer searches of ERIC's *Resources in Education* and *Current Index to Journals in Education.*

References

The ERIC documents cited in this section (items marked with an ED number) can be ordered through the ERIC Document Reproduction Service (EDRS) in Alexandria, Virginia or obtained on microfiche at more than 650 libraries across the country. For an EDRS order form, a list of libraries in your state that have ERIC microfiche collections, or both, please contact the ERIC Clearinghouse for Junior Colleges, 8118 Math-Sciences Building, UCLA, Los Angeles, California 90024.

Abbott, J. A. *Student Assessment Pilot Project: Maricopa County Community College District JCEP Project no. JZ-309, 1985-86.* Phoenix, Ariz: Maricopa County Community College District, 1986. 84 pp. (ED 270 154)

Beavers, J. L. *A Study of the Correlation Between English Qualifying Exam Scores and Freshman/Developmental English Grades at Wytheville Community College.* Report no. 83-1. Wytheville, Va.: Wytheville Community College, 1983. 9 pp. (ED 231 487)

Belcher, M. J. *A Cohort Analysis of the Relationship Between Entering Basic Skills and CLAST Performance for Fall 1981 First-Time-in-College Students.* Research Report no. 84-22. Miami, Fla.: Miami-Dade Community College, 1984a, 33 pp. (ED 267 870)

Belcher, M J. *Initial Transcript Analysis for a Sample of Students Who Failed Two or More Sections of the June 1984 CLAST.* Research Report no. 84-21. Miami, Fla.: Miami-Dade Community College, 1984b. 11 pp. (ED 256 450)

Belcher, M. J. *The Reliability of CLAST.* Research Report no. 84-19. Miami, Fla.: Miami-Dade Community College, 1984c, 32 pp. (ED 267 869)

Belcher, M. J. *Cumulative Grade Point Average and CLAST Performance for Fall 1984 Test Takers.* Research Report no. 85-09. Miami, Fla.: Miami-Dade Community College, 1985a. 10 pp. (ED 267 875)

Belcher, M. J. *Do Courses in English Improve Communication Performance on CLAST?* Research Report no. 85-03. Miami, Fla.: Miami-Dade Community College, 1985b. 16 pp. (ED 267 873)

Belcher, M. J. *The General Education Mathematics Curriculum and the CLAST.* Research Report no. 85-12. Miami, Fla.: Miami-Dade Community College, 1985c. 32 pp. (ED 256 452)

Belcher, M. J. *Improving CLAST Scores Through Attention to Test-Taking Strategies.* Research Report no. 85-02. Miami-Dade Community College, 1985d. 13 pp. (ED 267 872)

Belcher, M. J. *The Performance of English-as-a-Second-Language (ESL) Students on the Fall 1984 CLAST.* Research Report no. 85-14. Miami, Fla.: Miami-Dade Community College, 1985e. 16 pp. (ED 273 339)

Belcher, M. J. *The Role of Developmental Courses in Improving CLAST Performance.* Research Report no. 85-04. Miami, Fla.: Miami–Dade Community College, 1985f. 12 pp. (ED 267 874)

Belcher, M. J. *A Longitudinal Follow-Up of Students Who Failed the CLAST in Fall 1984.* Miami, Fla.: Miami–Dade Community College, 1986. 21 pp. (ED 273 340)

Belcher, M. J., and Losak, J. *Providing Educational Opportunity for Students Who Were Initially Ineligible to Enroll in the State University System.* Research Report no. 85-15. Miami, Fla.: Miami–Dade Community College, 1985. 9 pp. (ED 256 453)

Boggs, G. R. *The Effect of Basic Skills Assessment on Student Achievement and Persistence at Butte College: A Research Report.* Oroville Calif.: Butte College, 1984. 23 pp. (ED 244 686)

Borst, P. W., and Cordrey, L. J. *The Skills Prerequisite System, Fullerton College (A Six-Year Investment in People).* Fullerton, Calif.: North Orange County Community College District, 1984. 10 pp. (ED 255 247)

Bray, D. "Assessment and Placement of Developmental and High-Risk Students." In K. M. Ahrendt (ed.), *Teaching the Developmental Education Student.* New Directions for Community Colleges, no. 57. San Francisco: Jossey-Bass, 1987.

Bridges, J. B. "Fourteen Years of Assessment: Regents' Testing Program." Paper presented at the annual meeting of the Southeastern Conference on English in the Two-Year College, Memphis, Tenn., February 19-22, 1986. 9 pp. (ED 269 102)

Chand, S. "The Impact of Developmental Education at Triton College." *Journal of Developmental Education,* 1985, *9* (1), 2-5.

Cohen, A. M. "Helping Ensure the Right to Succeed: An ERIC Review." *Community College Review,* 1984-85, *12* (3), 4-9.

Cohen, A. M., and Brawer, F. B. *The Collegiate Function of Community Colleges: Fostering Higher Learning Through Curriculum and Student Transfer.* San Francisco: Jossey-Bass, 1987.

Digby, K. E. "The Use of the Language Usage Section of the Differential Aptitude Test as a Predictor of Success in Freshman-Level English Courses." Unpublished doctoral practicum, Nova University, 1986. 18 pp. (ED 269 098)

Forstall, J. C. *Survey of Assessment and Basic Skills in Illinois Public Two-Year Colleges.* Report no. 99. Springfield, Ill.: Lincoln Land Community College, 1984. 8 pp. (ED 248 927)

Friedlander, J. *Evaluation of Napa Valley College's Student Orientation, Assessment, Advisement, and Retention Program.* Napa, Calif.: Napa Valley College, 1984. 12 pp. (ED 250 026)

Haase, M., and Caffrey, P. *Assessment Procedures, Fall 1982 and Spring 1983: Semiannual Research Report, Part I.* Sacramento, Calif.: Sacramento City College, 1983. 89 pp. (ED 231 494)

Losak, J. *Relating Grade Point Average at Miami–Dade to Subsequent Student Performance on the College-Level Academic Skills Test (CLAST).* Research Report no. 84-03. Miami, Fla.: Miami–Dade Community College, 1984a. 8 pp. (ED 256 448)

Losak, J. *Success on the CLAST for Those Students Who Enter the College Academically Unprepared [and] Academic Progress of Students at Miami–Dade Who Were Initially Not Eligible to Enroll in the State University System.* Research Report nos. 84-04 and 84-30. Miami, Fla.: Miami–Dade Community College, 1984b. 13 pp. (ED 256 449)

Losak, J., and Morris, C. *Effects of Student Self-Selection into Remedial Classes.*

Research Report no. 83–39. Miami, Fla.: Miami–Dade Community College, 1983. 20 pp. (ED 239 679)

Loucks, S. *Diagnostic Testing: How Reliable in Determining Student Success Within Composition Class?* Seattle, Wash.: Shoreline Community College, 1985. 14 pp. (ED 273 321)

Miami–Dade Community College. *Miami–Dade Community College 1984 Institutional Self-Study.* Vol. II: *Prescriptive Education.* Miami, Fla.: Miami–Dade Community College, 1985. 118 pp. (ED 259 770)

Neault, L. C. *Phase II, The English Placement Test: A Correlation Analysis.* San Diego, Calif.: San Diego Community College District, 1984. 78 pp. (ED 245 725)

New Jersey Basic Skills Council. *Results of the New Jersey College Basic Skills Placement Testing, Fall 1985.* Trenton: New Jersey State Department of Higher Education, 1986. 71 pp. (ED 269 059)

Ramey, L. *Assessment Procedures for Students Entering Florida Community Colleges: Theory and Practice.* Gainesville: Florida Community Junior College Inter-institutional Research Council, 1981. 181 pp. (ED 231 474)

Rasor, R. A., and Powell, T. *Predicting English Writing Course Success with the Vocabulary and Usage Subtests of the Descriptive Tests of Language Skills of the College Board.* Sacramento, Calif.: American River College, 1984. 34 pp. (ED 243 535)

Richards, W. *The Effectiveness of New-Student Basic Skills Assessment in Colorado Community Colleges.* Denver: Colorado State Board for Community Colleges and Occupational Education, 1986. 33 pp. (ED 275 351)

Riley, M. *The Community College General Academic Assessment: Combined Districts, 1983–84.* Los Angeles: Center for the Study of Community Colleges, 1984. 59 pp. (ED 246 959)

Rivera, M. G. "Placement of Students in English Courses in Arizona Community Colleges, 1981." Paper presented to the Arizona English Teachers' Association and at the Pacific Coast Regional Conference on English in the Two-Year College, Phoenix, Ariz., November 6–7, 1981a. 8 pp. (ED 235 855)

Rivera, M. G. "Placement of Students in English Courses in Selected California Community Colleges." Paper presented to the Arizona English Teachers' Association and at the Pacific Coast Regional Conference on English in the Two-Year College, Phoenix, Ariz., November 6–7, 1981b. 14 pp. (ED 235 854)

Roberts, K. J. *The Relationship of ASSET Test Scores, Sex, and Race to Success in the Developmental Program, the Associate Degree-Level Programs, and the Associate Degree Programs in Business, Health, and Technology at MATC.* Basic Skills Assessment Reports 7861, 7862, and 11862. Milwaukee, Wis.: Milwaukee Area Technical College, 1986. 13 pp. (ED 275 374)

Rounds, J. C. "Assessment, Placement, Competency: Four Successful Community College Programs." Unpublished paper, 1984. 41 pp. (ED 241 080)

Rounds, J. C., and Andersen, D. "Assessment Procedures: What Works and What Needs Improvement in California Community Colleges?" Unpublished paper, 1984. 19 pp. (ED 252 255)

Santa Rosa Junior College. *DRT/ASSET/Final Grade Study. Fund for Instructional Improvement Final Report, 1983–84.* Santa Rosa, Calif.: Santa Rosa Junior College, 1984. 189 pp. (ED 253 272)

Spahr, A. E. *An Investigation of the Effect of Several Variables on Students' Grades in Rhetoric I and College Algebra.* Cicero, Ill.: Morton College, 1983. 8 pp. (ED 258 669)

Walvekar, C. C. "Section I: Evaluation of Learning: A Model for Developmental Education." In H. N. Hild (ed.), *Developmental Learning: Evaluation and Assess-*

112

ment. NARDSPE Research Report no. 1. Chicago: National Association for Remedial and Developmental Studies in Postsecondary Education, 1982. 52 pp. (ED 274 381; available in microfiche only)

Washington State Student Services Commission. *Student Assessment Task Force Report.* Olympia: Washington State Board for Community College Education, 1985. 28 pp. (ED 269 049)

Wiener, S. P. "Through the Cracks: Learning Basic Skills." *Community and Junior College Journal,* 1984-85, *55* (4), 52-54.

Wright, T. *The Effects of Increased Time Limits on a College-Level Achievement Test.* Research Report no. 84-12. Miami, Fla.: Miami-Dade Community College, 1984a.

Wright T. *Student Appraisal of College: The Second Miami-Dade Sophomore Survey.* Research Report no. 84-15. Miami, Fla.: Miami-Dade Community College, 1984b. 30 pp. (ED 267 868)

Jim Palmer is assistant director for user services at the ERIC Clearinghouse for Junior Colleges.

Index